HIS GRACE

IS SUFFICIENT

ELW Publications

HIS GRACE
IS SUFFICIENT

WILLIAM W. WASHINGTON, JR.

an autobiography

HIS GRACE IS SUFFICIENT

©2005 William W. Washington, Jr.

Library of Congress Control Number:
2005929236
ISBN: 0-9766233-0-7
Design: Mickey Moore Design Associates
www.mickeymoore.com

ELW Publications

P.O. Box 2862 • Charlottesville, VA 22902

Dedication

I dedicate this book to my wife, Joyce, a woman whom I love and adore. Every time I think of you, Joyce, my heart overflows with love, and I stand in amazement that God has blessed me with a beautiful, loving, and caring wife.

You complete me in so many ways. When I see my weakness, I look at you and you become my strength. And I pray every day, that by God's grace, I can become a better husband and a better servant.

Thank you for being my best friend, my companion, my lover. This book is a testimony of God's grace and his love through you to me.

Contents

Foreword

When I first saw William Washington, I was somewhat apprehensive. His eyes were without expression. They held a vacancy that said here was someone who could kill without remorse. As the guard left, the door clicked shut in our cinderblock interview room at the joint security complex, and it was just the two of us. I sensed the danger, but I also sensed that here was someone who was eager to know God.

Over the course of three years visiting the jail, I discovered a great yearning for spiritual growth on the part of the men incarcerated there. I befriended about forty-five men, and I was there long enough to see many of them get released only to return in a couple of months. In the pages of this book, you will find out about the only two I know who went on to lead productive lives. William is one of them.

I believe William's life answers two questions. The first is: What makes someone continue making progress in the face of relentless opposition? I saw every possible obstacle thrown in William's path, obstacles that would have discouraged anyone from continuing to make progress. Just as he would start to gain some momentum—every time it seemed as though he was going to make it—something from the past would reach out to try and drag him back into the old ways. Somehow he found a way through that was honorable.

The second question his life answers is: What reconciles people who would normally avoid each other? What turns "enemies" into friends? Through the work established by William and Joyce Washington, they have been able to engage the efforts of young and old, rich and poor, and black and white.

Both of their lives are evidence of the grace that does not give up, the grace that is more than sufficient for each and every one of us.

—John Manzano, Senior Pastor
Christ Community Church

Acknowledgments

There are a number of people I would like to thank. Many are frequently mentioned by name in the pages to come, but some have been more behind the scenes.

One person that comes to mind is Gary Greene. Gary, there are so many things I could say about your life that have made an impact on the story in this book. You have been there from the early days of this ministry, helping us to successfully take each step. You opened your life and your family to my wife and me, showing me that much-needed love, respecting me as a leader, and acknowledging the gifts I have been given. I am so grateful to call you my brother, my friend, but most of all, my leader. I believe I owe much of who I am as a leader today thanks to your leadership in my own life. You have been very kind, very gentle, and very giving. In times of turmoil and challenges, you have been a role model to me and others, displaying the right attitude and giving sound spiritual leadership and advice. You have faithfully served on our board for the last seven years, working to see God's goals for this ministry accomplished. In short, I believe you are a large part of the reason that we have a Bridge Ministry today.

Jeff and Susan Shane, thank you for the love and support you have given to this ministry and to my wife and me.

Thank you, Doug Horne, for the personal support and the encouragement you have given to my family and me as well as to this ministry.

To the men's group at First Presbyterian Church in Charlottesville, I can't say enough about the ways you have extended encouragement and friendship to me over the years. As I look back over many of the stories in this book, I see each one of you personally leading and guiding me. I want to thank you for that. And to the leadership of First Presbyterian, thank you for opening your hearts and your church up to me to allow me to see things from a whole different perspective.

To Garry Bryant and Russell James, thank you for believing in the vision.

Thank you, Rob Hewitt, for your support and help in writing this book.

Thanks also to Zenobia Joseph for being the mother to me that I never had and for helping Joyce and me understand how to live by God's Word.

Thanks to Keith Sherman and Jonathan Hornsby for their ongoing friendship and love, and for their support for the ministry.

And finally, to my four loving kids—Shanta, Waverly, Marquis, and Avanté—and to Gregory, my wonderful stepson, thanks for being a blessing in my life. I love each one of you dearly.

Preface

My grandfather was a white man who came from a long line of slave owners. My grandmother was Native American. In many ways, she was just another slave to him. My father, the result of this unhappy marriage, was looked down on by everyone in the neighborhood as a "half-breed." When he was fourteen, he married my mother, an African American.

I knew my father's god. He was a god who let you visit him on Sundays in church, but who would turn his head when you went around back and got drunk afterward with your friends. I knew my mother's god, a god you could talk about without letting him change you so others could see a difference. Deep inside, I knew there was a real God, a true God. He was pursuing me all along, but I had to seek him myself to finally find him.

This book is that story. Here is an opportunity for people who have doubts about God to know without a doubt that there is a God who can change lives. There is a God who forgives and heals. I am a witness to it. I am an example of what his love can do in the life of anyone who will come to him just as they are—helpless, hopeless, and with an open heart.

I don't care where you are, or what you're deal-

grace of God. It is something received that we do not deserve, and because of it we can have hope today. Don't be afraid to believe it. He is waiting to listen. His arms are not too small to hold us, nor too short to save. No matter what your need, his grace is sufficient.

Believe me, I know.

Why?

I remember talking to God. I was walking up the road. I don't know why (because I didn't have a clue who God was) but I said, "God, why can't I have a normal childhood? Just for once I would like to laugh and feel like a child—for just a moment." But I'd been trained not to allow myself to go there, that I had a responsibility. I couldn't think like that. "That's for four- and five-year-olds," I reminded myself, "not for seven-year-olds."

RAISED UP

PERSISTENT GRACE

CHAPTER ONE

DOWN HOME

When I was about ten years old, my father gave me a rifle, a chain saw, and an ax, and drove me about three miles into a wooded area. He cut a load of wood and told me to have the second load ready when he returned. Then he drove away and left me on my own.

I didn't feel bad about it, and I wasn't surprised. This was how I had been raised. Ever since I could remember, my father had been telling me about things like this that he had done growing up. So I knew the day was coming when I would enter into manhood and start providing for the family.

When he returned less than two hours later, I had the wood cut up and split, ready and waiting.

For the next few years I spent most of my time with my father. I went to school every now and then and I enjoyed it, but I was always behind. It wasn't that I couldn't learn or wasn't bright enough, it's just that I wasn't there enough to be able to keep up like I wanted. I had a thirst for knowledge, but I knew my father would take me out again to help provide for the family. Besides, even though my father had been rough with me, I loved him, and I loved being with him more than going to school.

I also knew my father loved me, even though he never said it out loud. He wasn't the kind of person who would give me a hug or let me sit on his lap. But he showed it in other ways, and I knew.

Education wasn't important to my father. Survival was.

Plantation Living

My father gave me everything he knew how to give as a father. He emptied himself of all the support and love he had known from his own childhood. But what he had been given was very little.

His own father—my grandfather—was a very wealthy man, a white man. He owned a large farm in Fluvanna County, Virginia, a rural area about a half hour from

Charlottesville and the University of Virginia. But just because my grandfather was wealthy didn't mean that life was easy for my father and his brothers.

My grandfather came from a long line of slave owners, and he seemed to have inherited the roughness and arrogance that often came with that position. He married a Native American woman. She was his wife in name, but in practice she was more or less his slave.

The same went for his boys, whom everybody in those days matter-of-factly called "half-breeds." At the age of seven, my father would get up at dawn to help feed the chickens and other farm animals—about three hours of work for him and his four brothers. Afterward they would all walk to school barefoot. Like most everybody else in the neighborhood, they wouldn't get a pair of shoes until the weather turned cold.

I remember my grandfather as an angry man. I don't think he ever once said hi to me. He didn't really say much to anyone. Though we lived only a mile away, he never came over to our house, but we did go over to his house every now and then.

Once when I was about four, all of us kids

were up in one of his enormous apple trees, where we loved to play. Grandpa didn't like us there, and he had told us to stay away, but it was so much fun to climb all over the big limbs. Well, that day Grandpa had had enough. He came outside, pointed his rifle toward us, and pulled the trigger.

We came down out of that tree like someone was shaking us out, and I ran home as fast as I could. "William!" I said, calling my father by his first name as I always did, still trying to catch my breath, "Grandpa shot at us!"

"Well, don't you go back over there," my father said, almost as if nothing had happened. "Grandpa will shoot you."

I couldn't understand why my grandfather treated us like that. In my little mind he was just an evil, mean-spirited man, and for years I was sure that all white people must be just like him.

Rustling Up Trouble

My father was fourteen when he married my mother, an African American girl three years older than himself. For about two years afterward, Grandpa disowned my father.

Even though Grandpa's sons didn't have a real place at the table in white society, he still didn't want any of them marrying a dark-skinned woman.

For a while, my father and mother lived in an abandoned house and made do the best they could. A year later my father was earning three dollars a week working at a sawmill. About the time my eldest sister was born, Grandpa softened a little and gave my father a small piece of land.

Our family was never wealthy, not by a long shot. But through my father's hard work, we managed to be one of the better-off families in our neighborhood. We never lacked for food, and we used to help support about three or four families besides our own.

But my father did have a problem with alcohol, and one night he decided to go cattle rustling with a couple of my uncles. Maybe they convinced him to go because they needed the truck he brought home from work every day. For some reason my mother went along too.

The whole little operation that night seemed to go without a hitch. My uncles killed the calf and threw it in the back of the truck. When they got back to our house, they took the calf out and butchered it right there in the backyard.

Unfortunately for my father, one of his check stubs had fallen on the ground where the calf had been taken. The next day the police found it and came looking for him. I was about six years old at the time, and I remember coming home from school and seeing the yard full of police cars. It was warm weather, and I was puzzled to see smoke pouring out of the chimney. I didn't know it then, but my uncles had tried to hide the evidence by burning the meat in our wood stove. I just stood there, watching in confusion as my father was led away, handcuffed.

My father didn't want to involve my uncles because my mother had also been in the car with them, so he took all the blame himself.

On the Run

My father had been in jail for a week when he came before the judge for his bond hearing. The judge set bail at fifty thousand dollars, a huge amount of money, and my mother, always faithful to my father, offered the house as a guarantee that he would show up for his court date.

It would be a couple of months before my father had to appear in court, and for a while things seemed as they had always been. But the day of his court appearance, he didn't show. The next day, the police came looking for him, but he was hidden back in the woods, concealed within a small shelter he had built out of brush. In the coming weeks, the police began showing up at the house at all hours, even at two o'clock in the morning. My father had to figure out a new plan, and we were a part of it. He took us anywhere he thought he could stay clear of the police, anywhere they wouldn't find us. Sometimes we left the county. A lot of times we slept in the woods beneath his brush shelter.

My mother set an example for us by how committed she was to serve him, even when my father was in trouble. We kids knew our father was head of the house. There was no questioning, either by us children or by our mother, what my father was doing. She followed my father wherever he went. She willingly left her home and took all of us out on the road to protect him.

After a few months of living like fugitives,

my father went up to Washington, D.C., where a lot of our family lived. He got a job and stayed out of trouble, but the police were still looking for him.

In the meantime, my mother had a fight on her hands. Since my father had skipped trial, the authorities wanted to take the house. My mother was determined she would not let that happen. I don't know how she did it, but she held on to that house, took care of us kids, and worked to make money, all the while going back and forth to D.C. to visit my father. She ran herself ragged for us and gave us confidence that she loved us and would always take care of us, no matter what.

One day my father decided to drive down from D.C. to visit us at home. The police had set up a roadblock that day—not for him, but to check everyone's state-inspection stickers to see if they were current. My father got caught in the line of traffic. There was no getting away for him then. They caught him, tried him, and put him in jail. He was going to be gone for a long time now. He would serve four years in the state penitentiary.

Little Man

There were seven of us kids still at home, from age four to sixteen. I was next to the youngest, but I was my father's only son. When my mother would take me to jail to see him, he would look at me and say, "You need to be the man of the house. You need to take care of your mother."

This wasn't just gentle-hearted encouragement. My father was serious. He meant I had to provide for the family. Even as a little boy, it was something I embraced—something I was always thinking about.

My father had put me on his "payroll" when I was about five, giving me a dollar a day to help him put firewood on the truck. I was little, but I did my share, and I learned how to work hard. I had also been responsible for cutting up the slab wood—the rounded parts of logs left over from milling—into pieces small enough to fit into our wood stove. We had a portable mill with a circular ripping blade powered by a tractor motor. As soon as I came home from school, I had to start up the mill and cut enough firewood to get us through the night. If I didn't finish before my father got home, I was afraid he might get angry and go into one of his rages. That's when he would physically abuse me. No one, not even those he loved, was safe then.

The winter after my father was arrested was one of the worst we had. There were about two or three feet of snow on the ground. We had no food in the house. The electricity had been cut off. There was no more wood for the stove. All of the slab wood my father had brought home was gone.

I had often watched my father use a chain saw. Now that I was seven and responsible for taking care of the family, I knew what I had to do. My father had built a barn in the back—some one-by-six-foot boards over a post frame. It wasn't hard work to cut through those boards, but I did have to hold the saw over my head to get the ones higher up. The danger of it didn't even occur to me. It was what I had to do to provide heat for the family.

My mother was working about an hour away at a building supply company, making about sixteen dollars a day. She was proud and didn't want to ask for help, but her husband was in jail, and there were few places left to turn. She went from house to house looking for help, but received nothing.

I remember one winter's night lying beside the wood stove. The power company had already turned off the electricity because we couldn't pay the bill. We couldn't pay the mortgage either, so we were going to lose the house soon. There was nowhere to go, and the snow was so deep—halfway up the door. I had cut up all the wood I could get from the barn, and there was nothing left to burn.

I looked into the corner where we usually stacked the wood. "Mom," I said. "It's cold. We don't have any firewood." She looked so tired.

Slowly she got up and went into her room, emerging with an armful of summer dresses. Coming back to where we were huddled, she knelt down, opened the door to the wood stove, and one by one fed her dresses into the fire to keep it going. As I watched her, my heart was very sad. Even as a little boy, I could see the weight upon her. But though our surroundings looked like we were defeated, in my mother I saw hope.

My mother was the backbone of our family. Not only could she provide for us as a mother, she could provide for us as a father. She made trip after trip into town, fighting with the mortgage company and the courts in order to hold on to our house. Somehow, by sheer persistence and determination, she won. For the time being, at least, we had a place to stay.

Driving Lessons

For my part, over the next four years my father was in jail, I did what I could to help out. One way I provided for the family was by fishing. There was a pond nearby—someone else's, where I wasn't supposed to be—and in a few hours I could catch enough brim, crappie, and small bass to make a meal for our family. I brought them home and cleaned them, and my mother fried them up. That, along with a salad made from "wild greens," would be our main meal for the day.

When my father was released from jail, I was eleven years old, but my role as family provider would not end. If anything, I was expected to do more. My test in the woods—alone with rifle, chain saw, and ax—was only the beginning.

One thing my father's schedule of hard

work did for me was help keep me out of a lot of the trouble going on in our neighborhood. I remember some of the things the kids would do when they were going off to parties and clubs—stealing, rebelling, lying. By keeping me working, he was, in his own way, protecting me from the wild side of life. And that was fine with me, because I wanted to spend time with him too.

For a while, my father drove a truck for a paving company. We left the house together about two or three o'clock in the morning, and sometimes he'd let me drive. The practice came in handy. Many times I had to drive my father home from my cousin's house, or from the gambling hall or the pool hall, because he was too intoxicated to drive himself. At ten, I was barely able to see over the steering wheel, but I still drove that old, three-speed Chevy pickup many, many miles—sometimes in the dark.

Though my father's work ethic kept me out of a lot of trouble, he brought some trouble home to me. Every so often he would present me with a bag of marijuana. It was his way of showing his love, a special gift for his young helper. Like my father, I never really understood the danger.

The 'Hood

Even though I was heavily involved in smoking marijuana from the time I was eleven, to me it was something very normal. After all, my father had given me the okay to do it. I kept trying to get into some more things of that sort, but in the country back then, it seemed there was only so much trouble you could get into. We had a little gang that got together to cause mischief and generally annoy people. But mostly, whether they knew it or not, the older folks around us taught us the "lessons" we would never forget.

Every Friday night in our country neighborhood was a time of violence. I saw my stepbrother get shot by my uncle. I watched my uncle get shot six times and killed by my first cousin. I saw my father shoot a man, and I watched him beat men until they were unconscious. We would kill each other, but we would defend the area against any intruders. We were so fierce, that one time some law enforcement officers came in and had to leave on foot, abandoning their cars. These were the scenes of my childhood.

My father taught me to never let a man do

anything to me. If they did, I should do what-ever it took to defend myself—even kill them if necessary.

When I was about eleven, my cousin and I got into a fight. It got pretty bad, so I took off running to the house and grabbed my father's rifle. Just as I headed out the door, my moth-er saw me and shouted to my father, "William's got the gun!"

Coming quickly, my father grabbed me.

"What's going on?"

I was so angry all I could say was, "I'm gonna kill him. I'm gonna kill him."

"Kill who?"

I told him it was my cousin.

He just looked at me and said, "You can't shoot him because he's my brother's son."

He was not concerned that I was getting ready to shoot someone; he was just con-cerned about who I was going to shoot.

I gave him the gun, and I calmed down.

If my father hadn't caught me going out the door, I know I would have killed my cousin that day. That was just the expected thing to do. That night my father took me to where my cousin was hanging out with a group of his friends, and I finished the fight there. My father didn't want me to kill my cousin, but he did want me to hurt him. As a family, we were very serious about revenge.

That was my life, and I never let my thoughts go beyond where I lived. I really couldn't even imagine anything else. There was no one around me trying to improve their condition or build their lives. Even my father was just surviving, trying to keep hold of what he had. My world was filled with people in bondage, people who were trapped in a miserable little world and blind to the possibility of anything better. They had lived in garbage so long that they had lost their sense of smell. I was never challenged about how I lived or what I did. Before that ever happened, I would sink a lot deeper.

Shoot and Run

My mother tried to motivate me—at least a little every now and then—to get my school-work done. She had received very little education herself, and one particular night she seemed especially insistent. The teacher had gotten in touch with her. I was fourteen now and hadn't been doing any schoolwork at all because I was working with my father. "You really need to get your work done," she urged.

My youngest sister—who was just a baby—had taken my writing tablet and used up the paper to play with. I didn't have anything to do my homework on, and I was fussing with my mother about this when my father walked in. He had been drinking. He arrived just in time to see me angrily snatch the tablet from my baby sister, who had now begun crying loudly.

"Give it back to her," my father said, an angry snarl in his voice.

"No!" I stood my ground. "This is for my homework."

That was the first time in my life that I had ever said "no" to my father or even raised my voice to him. As soon as the words were out of my mouth, I knew I was in serious trouble.

Mumbling something, my father turned and went outside. Instinctively, I followed him. Something bad was going to happen, and I wanted to protect my mom and sister from whatever he might do.

Going over to the truck, he pulled out his gun. When he turned back around, I was facing him, planted between him and the house. Moving toward me, he met my gaze. He fired the gun once, twice, blindly aiming at the lower half of my body. He's trying to scare me, I thought, and I stayed where I was, not wanting to run. He kept coming, his eyes locked on mine. A third time he pulled the trigger wildly, and a bullet pierced the top of my foot.

For a while, he just stood there and looked at me. No longer able to stand, I turned and began hopping toward the house. Reaching the porch, I sat down and faced him once again. It was then I saw it. I had seen it before when he had beaten my mother and we children had to hide in the house or run to the neighbors. I had seen it when he had hurt someone or shot at them. And I was seeing it now as he looked straight at me—that rage, that uncontrolled, unpredictable anger.

He was coming toward me again, and I was sure he planned to kill me.

The sound of the gunshots had brought my mother and sister out onto the front porch. "What have you done?" my mother screamed at him. At once, as if called from a deep trance, my father stopped. Something had pulled him back to his senses. The rage was over. Picking me up like a baby, he put me in the truck and carried me to the hospital.

While I was there, my mother came to me alone and crying. There was a policeman outside my hospital room door, waiting to ask me some questions. "William, tell them the truth," my mother told me. "I'm not asking you to protect your father."

I remember my father's face when he visited me. My father was my "god." He was my whole world and I loved him dearly. When the policeman came in, he asked, "What happened, son?"

"I was cleaning the gun," I replied simply, "and it misfired."

No one asked me to say that. I just didn't want to see my father go to jail again. He had suffered there, and I knew it, but my mother had suffered even more. I could still close my eyes and watch her feeding her dresses into the wood stove to keep us warm. I would not let that happen again, not if I could help it.

Two days after I got home from the hospital, I took a knife and cut the cast off. I wrapped some tape tightly around my foot, put a shoe over it, and left my home for good.

No Looking Back

Sometimes when I think about what I had to go through, I get a little angry, but it does not last long. I've asked, "Why did I have to go through all that?" I would have loved to have gone to college and lived a normal life. Why couldn't I have had that opportunity for education?

I can't remember any time during my childhood that I could look back on and say, "That was a good time in my life." I worked. I ate. I slept. In between those times, I had to fend for myself and keep clear of my father's rage. I had nothing in my background that would even let me imagine how my kids would grow up today. I was a kid trying to live like a man at the age of ten.

This may sound strange, but many years later I came to the conclusion that I wouldn't trade any of my past for where I am today. What I have received is more valuable than education, more valuable than anything else I would have chosen, because now I have something that will last.

Many people have lost hope. It's even worse now than when I was growing up. But it doesn't matter how bad or how hard the things are that you're going through today. I want you to know that there is always hope. I found it, and when I did, I held on for dear life.

CHAPTER TWO

CITY WAYS

Hobbling along the roadside, I eventually managed to catch a few rides to Charlottesville, the nearest large town. I arrived there homeless, broke, and in a lot of pain. When the bullet entered my foot, it had broken a bone, and of course I hadn't given it time to heal. Added to that, the bullet hadn't been removed.

A couple of my sisters lived in town, but I didn't want to risk the chance that they would tell my father where I was. I didn't want to see my father anymore. I was going to have to make it on my own. My first thought was to get among other African Americans. If anyone would help me, they would. I went over to a housing project, but I soon found out how things were. If you didn't live there, you weren't accepted there. After a few "encounters," I tried the other housing project in town, but it was the same story. Charlottesville was turning out to be a very segregated place.

By the time I made my way over to Main Street, the sun had gone down. As I watched, drug addicts, drug dealers, and alcoholics started to come out of their daytime hiding. I had grown up in a rough and violent place, but this would turn out to be a whole new world to me, with a whole new set of rules.

My first night on the streets, I started talking to some dealers. They told me how I could make money working for them. And I did it to survive.

After I got to know some of the dealers better, they would let me sleep at their place. Eventually, I did wind up staying with one of my sisters from time to time. I lived anywhere I could, anywhere somebody would take me in.

I remember not having any food. Maybe there was a soup kitchen in town then, maybe not. I was from the country, and I had no idea that something like that was even a possibility. Every night after McDonald's closed, they would throw their leftover food in the dumpster. That was my soup kitchen.

When I was in need and just wanting something to eat, I had a tendency to take any favor that was offered me, but every favor came with a cost. A drug dealer will try to buy you. They'll pay you for your time and give you the things you need, just to use you as a pigeon.

Everything I learned, I learned the hard way.

Night Sounds

I had no sense of security—no food, no roof over my head, no mother or father to give me these things. All of that had vanished overnight. Everything that had been familiar to me during my first fourteen years was gone, even my sleeping and waking. Drug dealers and addicts are like the fictitious zombies of a late-night horror movie—they sleep during the day and come out at night. When the first light of dawn appears, they go back inside to their own darkness.

That became my way of seeing the world, too, and I was almost always afraid. Each night brought its own dangers. I had to watch carefully and learn. Mistakes were costly. At first I didn't know that dealers had their territories, that if you sold drugs or even picked up money in their area, you were in trouble. After I was beaten up two or three times, I took up boxing and karate just to protect myself. I became pretty good at it.

My job for the dealers was to meet a customer driving up in their car, then exchange the drugs for payment. Most people using the type of drugs we were selling didn't have a lot of money. There was always the chance they would take the drug and shoot the delivery boy, or maybe just speed away before they paid. If I didn't bring the money back to the dealer, I would be in serious trouble. Every time a strange car drove up, I had to make a quick decision. Was this the police? Would these people rob me? Kill me? I had to take a chance. Survival had no margins.

After a while, it became easier to tell which cars contained customers. I was dealing for people who were serious about their work, and I was learning quickly. As far as I was concerned, I had no other choice. I did not know how to hustle. I was living in a jungle full of predators—and my job was to keep from becoming their prey.

Lost

In a word, I was lost. I didn't have a friend, no one to really talk to. Going back home was out of the question. After what my father had done, I was sure he didn't love me. There was nowhere to go. I was just wandering.

There was one thing that I brought from the country that helped me survive. Ironically, it was a gift from my father—endurance. When I first came to the city, there were a lot of things I didn't know how to do and had never even seen before. Instead of walking away from them as obstacles, I saw them as opportunities. My attitude was like this: If you give me a chance, and show me how, I can do this. I can do anything.

Just like my father had taught me, I was taking on a man's responsibility. To my amazement, I quickly realized that I was around grown men who didn't understand this basic principle of working at something until you got good at it. As a result, even at fourteen, I felt that I was among equals. More than that, I knew that drug dealing was not just something I could learn; it was something I could master.

There were two important ways I could

benefit any dealer willing to hire me. First, they could trust me—at least to a certain extent. I had been raised to be honest and respectful, and essentially that's the way I was toward them. I said, "Yes, sir," and "No, sir," and took every responsibility seriously.

The second way I benefited dealers was that I gave them a wide profit margin. With me out there on the front lines, at the point of sale, they could still make their money while keeping their risks at a minimum. Besides, I worked cheap—room and board and a little spending money. I was the perfect pigeon.

Abandoned

One night I remember clearly. It was snowing outside and very, very cold. I didn't really have any shoes. What I wore on my feet had holes so big I may as well have been barefoot.

One of my sisters had moved into town, so I decided to go to her place to find shelter for the night. She was family, and that counted for something. Trudging up to her house, I knocked on the door, but there was no answer. It was locked, and I could hear her friends up in the house drinking and partying.

One of them looked down and saw me.

"It's your brother," he said.

My sister knew that I had people who wanted to kill me, so she never knew what type of trouble I was bringing behind me. I knocked again, louder. Still, no one came to the door. I knocked as hard as I could, until my knuckles ached with cold. But it was no use. They weren't going to let me in. I was left to spend the night outside, shivering like some forgotten stray.

Months later, my sister came looking for me with some bad news. My mother had died. I was sixteen years old, and it hit me pretty hard.

In many ways, my mother's understanding of life had been the same as my father's. She had been forced to grow up quickly, helping to raise her six sisters after her own mother had died. When I lived at home, my mother worked all the time. In addition to other work she could find, she spent twenty-two years doing housekeeping for the same lady. My mother worked hard until the day she died.

With her gone, everything was over for me. There was nobody else I knew who loved me. I had no protection left, no security. Something inside me changed. I was angry—very angry—especially at God. I couldn't be a pigeon any more. Pigeons were just prey. I had to become the predator.

Cracked

It wasn't long before I got my first jail sentence. I can't even remember what it was for. When I got out, I started doing the same things again, and that of course meant getting high.

There was a guy I used to hang out with who used some pretty heavy drugs, mostly ones you had to inject into your veins. I used to watch him all the time, but I stuck with marijuana. Maybe I didn't like the thought of sticking myself with a needle. One night, he had something a little different, a white powder that you just sniffed up through your nose.

He looked over at me and asked, "Do you want a hit?" I did. It was cocaine, and I liked it.

At first, cocaine was just a party drug, something I used occasionally on a Saturday night to get high. Like marijuana, though, it was a lead-in to something worse in my life, another type of cocaine known as "crack."

We didn't know anything about crack until some out-of-town dealers came in with it. At first, they would just give it away. That's how I got started. I even helped them pass out their "free samples." But like everything else in this drugged-up world I was living in, the favor came with a price. These dealers knew their bait, and they were fishing in a stocked pond.

I have experienced many drugs during my life, but I have never experienced anything like crack cocaine. I have seen decent, honest people become liars and bums overnight. The first five or six times you do crack, it seems like the best "high" you've ever had. Even though you've seen other people whose lives are wasted from this drug, you convince yourself that it will never happen to you. But even as you're swallowing this lie, you're choking on the hook that will grab you forever.

Hard Ball

The high I used to get from a joint of marijuana would last two to three hours, maybe the whole day. But I could smoke a hit of crack up in five minutes and want more right away. And each hit would cost up to fifty dollars.

Crack takes away your appetite. On crack you can go without eating for three or four days and never even know you are close to death. Your strength is gone. You walk around like a dead man, looking for the next hit—always wanting, always needing—never satisfied. The weekend drug soon became a Monday drug, a Tuesday drug, a Wednesday drug. . . .

I've seen a 200-pound man on crack go down to 130 pounds in one month. I carried a smaller frame in those days, but I still went from 130 to 105. I couldn't keep a job. I was hardly hanging on to life.

I understood that if I was to survive, things had to change. I needed cash—lots of it—to be able to get the drug that was now clawing at me, driving me. Drug dealing was like a regular job to me, and like everything else I did, I set out to become the best. I became good at taking people's money, good at hurting people. I strategized how to make it better, how I could discipline people so I could get what I wanted out of them. It didn't matter that I only weighed 105. I knew what I had to do, and I did it. I had seen this type of violence every weekend when I was growing up. Now it was just a matter of putting it into practice.

I was now at a whole different level. In addition to boxing and karate, I carried a choice of firearms and other weapons. My heart had grown hard and lifeless. I had no mercy. When I hurt someone, I didn't feel for them. I knew what the selling was doing. I'd watched mothers give me the money they needed for their kids' groceries. All of this used to bother me in the beginning. Now it was all about me, all about playing the game. The ones who learn how to play it learn how to survive. I learned how to play it and play it well.

Selling drugs not only paid for the drugs I needed, it also took care of my basic needs. I was a "provider" again. The way I saw things, I was a success. I thought I was taking a step up, but it was really a step down.

Soul Mate

Not long before my twenty-first birthday, I met an eighteen-year-old girl named Joyce. There was something special about Joyce, a certain beauty and kindness. I felt a freedom to be myself with her, something I had never known before—not with anyone. I believed this was someone I wanted to spend the rest of my life with. That wasn't the way things usually went for me. I had had a lot of relationships with women, and I wasn't looking for anything different. But somehow I sensed this young woman was my "soul mate."

As it had for me, Joyce's "adulthood" had begun at a very early age. She was still struggling with a lot of those things from her past. But even in this process, I could see an intelligent woman with a lot of talent and potential. She was a flower about to bloom, and with the right opportunities, she could become a rose. Somehow, I knew I wanted to be a part of her life.

Joyce was still living with her parents when we met. She had a son, Gregory, who was two years old. Joyce never saw the man I was becoming. She never knew about my addiction or how rough I was. I never let her see that side of me, because I knew that if she did, she would probably walk away.

After about a year or more, when Joyce had given me a "trial period," we moved into an apartment together. Life changed for me then. Here was someone I could give my life to. Now I had a purpose beyond me, and beyond the drugs. I felt I had come to a place in my life that I had been groomed for—to be a husband, a father, and the provider of my home. To have this opportunity to share with Joyce made my life worth living.

Encouraged by this new sense of direction, I tried to clean up my act a little. A local car dealership hired me as a detailer—someone who carefully cleaned and polished cars. Before long, I discovered that detailing could be taken to a completely different level, and I was intrigued. My employer sent me to Richmond to take some classes, and I returned to Charlottesville as the only certified detailer in town. Things were going well, but I knew that I could do even better financially if I started my own business. After a few months, I left the dealership and ventured out on my own.

Business was great. I was working in upper-class neighborhoods detailing Porsches, Lamborghinis, you name it. By working just three to four days a week I could profit about $2,500 a month—pretty good take-home pay for those days. My confidence was soaring.

Death Wish

My sudden success in the business world blinded me to what was really going on in my heart. I didn't realize that my increased income was really setting me up to go deeper into a life of bondage. I figured I had my crack habit under control. But I soon learned differently.

One night I had a dream that I was fighting the drug. Something was trying to force it on me. I hollered, "No!" But it wouldn't stop. Again and again I screamed, "No!" Suddenly I woke up. It was about 2 a.m. Joyce was asleep. I was alone, without strength, without anyone to help me. I knew I had lost control. I was a slave to this thing, and there was nothing I could do to get free.

Eventually, I gave up trying.

Over time, Joyce's endurance finally ran thin, too. She grew tired of my ups and downs, my irresponsibility, my days away from the apartment. There was more to think about than the two of us. In addition to her son, Gregory, Joyce and I had a new baby of our own, Shanta. I know that the cares of being a mother without a dependable father weighed heavily on her. Basically, she was raising those kids by herself. I wasn't there enough to make a difference.

One day, I walked back into the apartment, and as soon as Joyce saw me, she knew I was high. I saw the hopelessness in her eyes. The things we had worked for together were slipping away. The drugs were taking it all, and she didn't want to wind up as one of the losses.

In the past, Joyce had seen me working hard for her and for the kids. She knew that if I had to stay up until midnight working an extra job, I would make sure I provided for the needs of the family. I think she wanted to shock me back into responsibility.

"I'm sick and tired of all this," she told me. "Throw those drugs away, or I'm leaving."

There was no one I loved more than her and the kids, but what was the use? I knew I couldn't win against the drugs.

"Well, go ahead then," I told her. "Leave."

Joyce was stunned. She had no idea how strong a hold those drugs had on my life. Now, she was seeing the reality of this addiction for the first time. She just stood there, tears filling her eyes.

For some reason, though, Joyce stayed.

Many times afterward I said the words, "I have to get off these drugs," and I tried. I really tried. But it only lasted a few days. Day after day, things just got worse and worse.

One night I came into the apartment having spent all our money on drugs. Joyce was lying there asleep, pregnant with our third child. Shanta, now two, was lying beside her. They needed so much, and I had nothing to give them.

I knew I had a responsibility. I had taken care of my own family from the time I was seven, but now I was failing miserably. Endurance had been my sole strength. Now, even that was gone.

And then I said, "I can't do this any more."

Walking over to the medicine cabinet, I opened each bottle and swallowed every single pill they contained. Then I went to the gas cooking stove and blew the pilot light out. Putting a sheet over my head, I inhaled all the gas I could until I couldn't stand it any more. Just before I passed out, I said to myself—but out loud—"Thank God it's over."

Soft Love

I had come to the city a naïve, fourteen-year-old, lost and wandering. Oddly enough, I still had the politeness and country manners of my upbringing. And I hurt when I saw others in pain. In just a few years, all of that changed. I became a hardened man, ready to hurt, to do whatever it took to get the money, to get the drug.

Looking back, I can see that when my mother died, as far as I was concerned, love died with her. Love keeps your heart soft. Once you feel like you've lost that, you put your heart in a shell. The evidence of love is still there, but now it's hidden.

I never dealt with my mother's death; I was able to keep it buried within me by drinking and using drugs. I actually despised drinking—I never wanted to be like my father—so I mostly chose a different drug. I was setting myself up in a different way.

I've noticed especially that men can seem to get along fine without love. It's like we're designed to be on our own for long periods of time. We can fake the absence of love for a while, but then we collapse. Yes, we men are a unique species when it comes to setting ourselves up.

Of course, it's not just men who find themselves with a hardened heart. Anyone—a child, a teenager, a young woman—anyone who has been starved of love seeks out ways to protect themselves from the hurt and the emptiness.

Joyce brought love back for a while. I loved her, or thought I did. In reality I knew little of what it meant to truly love someone. I was selfish and self-serving, but I tried to love by providing what she and the children needed. That was my father's way, and it was my way too.

But this kind of love would not take me out of the tailspin I was in. It was not strong enough. It was only a distraction, a cheap imitation. What I needed was something to make my heart soft again, a love that would bring life back into me.

It had to be soon. I was running out of time.

not only a drug dealer, I was a drug chaser, and my need for the drug started putting me in dangerous places.

The people I dealt with were hardened and ruthless. We were not just getting high, we were walking around with guns like gangsters, ready to do whatever we had to do to defend ourselves—making that money, getting that drug. Some out-of-town dealers killed a drug dealer I worked with, and they had tried to kill others. Now it was easy to see what this game had always been: a matter of life and death.

I had an intense hatred for people coming from out of town to sell drugs. This was my territory. They were the intruders. So I played a very dangerous game. When they first got into town, I would earn their trust by selling about one thousand dollars' worth of drugs for them. In the process, I'd find out how much they brought with them and who their dealers were. At night, when the dealers were on the streets, I would go and take what I wanted.

When you're a drug dealer, you can't trust anyone, not even your best friend. It's all about the drugs, not about friendship or honor. These New York dealers were hard and cold. They had already killed two of the guys I associated with, and it didn't take long before they caught on to my game. I would be their next target.

Word got out and I tried to stay out of sight, but one night I was really wanting a high. I got a friend of mine to give me a ride in his pickup truck so I could purchase some drugs. This way, I thought, I could get in and out of there without being seen.

The dealer I was planning to buy from that night was someone who had sold for me. What I didn't know was that he had recently started working for the out-of-town dealers. Just the night before, I had completed one of my burglaries, and they probably told him that very day that they were looking for me. It was payback time. The pickup turned into a secluded alleyway connecting two streets and came to a stop.

The alleyway was dark. So were the spaces between the several houses on both sides. I got out of the truck on the passenger's side. As I handed the dealer the money, I sensed that something wasn't right. He was staring at something over my shoulder.

Quickly I looked to my left and saw one of the out-of-town dealers running toward me. I heard some people cry, "Gun!" Everyone around me started to move. Now I saw a second dealer closing in from behind. Both of them had their guns drawn.

As soon as I saw them, I took off running. I began waving frantically to my friend in the pickup who had begun to accelerate as fast as he could, trying to get away himself. When the truck came close, I jumped over the tailgate and into the back. "Keep going!" I hollered at him, pounding on the back window. The truck flew out of the alley, onto the street and away. I looked anxiously behind me, but they were not following. I was safe. For some reason, I was spared. That night, they were going to kill me.

Jail Time

There were four of us dealers who worked together. Everyone was killed except me. Joyce never knew the danger, but she wouldn't see me sometimes for a week. When I felt like the drug dealers were close to killing me, I wouldn't come home. I didn't want to have her or the kids getting hurt. When things calmed down, I'd come home for a few days, then I'd leave again.

I wound up being sent to jail several times—three months, six months, a year—each time serving about a third of the sentence. Each time I walked through those iron doors, the same chaplain came up to me—out of all the people there—and said, "Son, do you know Jesus Christ as your Lord and Savior?"

I said, "Old man, get away from me! Leave me alone. Go and mess with all those other guys. I don't know Jesus Christ and I don't want to get to know him."

He just replied, "That's okay. That's okay."

The next time I went in to serve time, the chaplain came to me again. I said to myself, This man is crazy!

He said, "You need Jesus," but all I could say was, "You need some help. You really need some help."

That wasn't the last time he would try to tell me about Jesus, and before long I would be listening.

Drive-In Drive-By

One time after being released I went to

Louisa, a rural county south of Charlottesville, where we set up a kind of "drive-in." A group of us were at one location, where we would take the drug orders and radio them ahead to the pick-up spot. The car would drive up a little farther and exchange the cash for drugs.

As one particular group drove up, one of the guys with us started to get agitated. He began yelling at somebody in the car, pointing his finger at him and cursing. It was obvious they had had an earlier confrontation that was far from over. The order was placed, and the car moved on, but the yelling didn't stop.

Without any warning, one of the men on the passenger's side of the car fired a shot backward over his shoulder in our general direction. There was no time to react. As the gun went off, I heard the bullet whizzing past my ear. Any closer, and it would have gone through my head.

"Thank you, Lord," I heard myself say to my own surprise. I didn't even know this God, but I found myself calling to him again.

When I laid down that night to go to sleep, the words I had spoken would not be silent. Over the next several days, they became a puzzling but persistent witness to me. Was there a God? Yes, I felt like there was, but, if so, what was he like? He had gotten my attention. What I didn't know was that I was headed to the basement of my life to find him.

Shadow Caster

Word came to me that there were some new dealers in town, so I made plans to rob them. It had been three days since I had eaten or slept. I know my six-foot, 105-pound frame may have looked pathetically harmless, but I was ready to protect myself by any means necessary.

As I made my way to the new dealers, I decided to take a shortcut through the graveyard. Suddenly, I saw the shadows of men at the top of the hill.

Okay, I said to myself. This is it. It's over. They're gonna kill me because of what I've done to them. But I'm not running or hiding. I want out. Lifelessly, I started straight toward them.

In the blink of an eye, the shadows moved from fifty feet away to right in front of me. Was I hallucinating? I looked over in the graveyard. Shadows were everywhere.

Though it was very dark, these shadows were darker than dark, and moving as fast as light.

I knew there was no use pulling a gun. I was in a realm beyond my understanding. Everywhere I turned, there were shadows. They surrounded me. Fear caught at my throat, and I began to run as fast as I could.

I reached my sister's house and began beating on the door with both fists, screaming with what breath was left in me. When the door opened, I ran upstairs and jumped into a corner. I didn't move for some time, except for the trembling of my body. I knew that I had been seeing something more than the physical world around me. Death was close to me. It had come so close that it had scared me back into reality.

The next morning, I turned myself in to the police. They had an arrest warrant out for me. Once again the chaplain paid me a visit. I know I didn't respond like he wanted me to, but he had my attention now. I believe I had seen something in the spiritual realm, something that seemed evil and beyond my understanding, and I was listening for some answers.

Life in the Hearse

I spent about a year in jail on that charge, and while I was there I said to myself over and over and over again, *I am going out, and I'm gonna get a job. I'm getting off these drugs. I'm not coming back.* But the very day I got out, I went straight back to the drug—the very drug I'd fought against all that time. And I didn't just go back—I was led back to it. I was controlled. I had no resistance when it came to this drug. I had to go back.

As soon as I was released, I headed for the country. I supposed I always felt more at home there, but now that place was infested with drugs. Some members of my family had monopolized the area's drug traffic, and all the drugs going into Charlottesville were being funneled through their territory.

I hadn't slept for four days. My mind became so tired. I was fed up with my life, and I wanted to die. In fact, I was looking for an opportunity to die. *Anything is better than this life.* Just then, to my surprise, up pulled a long, shiny black car. At first, I thought it was a hearse.

No one knew this car, and for a while everybody just stood there looking at it.

Panicking, someone yelled, "Police! Run!" But just as we were turning away, a man stepped out with a Bible in his hand. Two older ladies were with him.

As soon as he got out he said, "I'm not the police."

All three of them began to walk among us, talking about God. The man with the Bible came up to me and said, "Brother, you know God loves you."

I didn't tolerate too many people back then. When you're dying, you don't have to. But there was something about him that caught my attention.

I said, "Pastor, I don't want to be disrespectful, but you're wasting your time here. Go talk to somebody who has some hope, because there's none here. I'm a dead man. I know I'm going to die."

He looked at me, and he knew I meant every word. I wasn't just trying to put him off. He heard the hopelessness in my voice, but he looked back with compassion in his eyes.

"Son," he repeated, "God loves you. God can help you."

I just looked back at him with those empty

eyes of mine.

Turning around, he got back in the car and the three of them drove away. I never saw that man again, but in my heart I know he prayed for me.

God Money

Throughout these desperate months of my life, there were always little encouragements to keep my heart open. And they had their effect. One day I was invited to a Sunday morning church service by Esther Thorne, a woman who worked in the jail and who had started spending some time with Joyce. I was a little nervous about going in, but the place didn't remind me of the church I had gone to as a young boy. They were meeting in a school, which may have made it easier for me as a newcomer, and the music was pretty lively, which didn't hurt either.

The pastor was reading from the Bible, and he talked about people being wounded and rejected. It reminded me of my own wounds and the separation from my family. Before I knew it, I found myself doing something that was very unfamiliar to me—I began to cry. I had been taught all my life never to show any emotion or hurt, but, for some reason I didn't understand, my heart just melted.

After the meeting was over, someone I'd never seen came up to me.

"I felt like God wanted me to give this to you," he said, and he handed me some money.

Ordinarily I would have used a "hand out" like that to buy drugs, but there was something special about this gift. To me, it symbolized something good in my life, and I had to do right with it. This was so unlike me, because nothing was more important to me than drugs, not even my family. I wound up using every last cent of that gift for food, with one exception: I bought a pack of cigarettes. And that bothered me. It bothered me a lot.

Not long afterward, I was in jail again. The same chaplain just kept coming and coming. He was persistent, and I learned that he was real. As a con artist, I could tell the real thing from a fake. One of the things that got my attention about this man was the love and concern he showed for all of us. Over about a month's time, I got to trust him. One day he called me into his office, and after we talked, he led me in a prayer to ask Jesus Christ to be the Lord of my life. He said it would help my addiction. It was a little awkward. I didn't know what it meant completely, but it seemed like the right thing to do. He called it prayer. For me, it was more like a ritual we went through. I had a need. I was looking for any answers.

One Step at a Time

The chaplains in jail helped a lot, but the person who made the biggest impression on me was someone who didn't even have to come to the jail, a local pastor named John Manzano.

Just like some of the big-time dealers I had learned to hate and rob, John was a Hispanic from New York City who grew up in the projects. But that's where the similarities ended. He was a pastor at Christ Community Church, where I had wept listening to the Bible that Sunday.

For a while, all of the inmates tested John to see if he was genuine, if he lived what he talked about. He used to call three or four people into one of the white cinder-block meeting rooms, and we would talk with him back and forth, studying the first ten chapters of a book in the Bible called Proverbs.

Even though John was from a different background than the rest of us, we knew there was something special about him. He was not there on his own mission. You could hear the truth in what he said.

Two more times I was released and then returned to jail. Each time, John came back to visit me. That's when he got my attention. *This is the third time I've been in here, and he's still willing to spend time with me.* Now I opened up my heart. I listened. And I believed. There was nothing he could tell me that I didn't believe. What he shared spoke of the truth, and that's what I needed in my life.

Every week when John came, several of us would go to the meeting. One was a huge man, about six feet six, 250 pounds—a boxer, and a good one. When we were with John, the man would say, "God this" and "God that," but when we got back to the cell block, he would torment us.

John, however, was given insight about him, and one day confronted him. "I'm wasting my time with you," John said plainly. After that, John stopped calling him out. I, on the other hand, was still going to the meetings, so I became the focus of the boxer's anger.

Each time I came back to the cell, trouble was waiting. He and a group of his friends would try to annoy us when we prayed, or they would play some childish prank. Once or twice, he even stole my food tray. If I didn't fight, I wouldn't eat. And I refused to fight. It wasn't that I was afraid of him. I still had my limits, and he knew it. But I understood now that God was peaceful and had come to earth as a humble man. I wanted that change in my life.

For the first time, I was beginning to understand there was something—no, someone—more powerful, more lasting, and more gracious than I had ever thought possible. Here was someone who could lead me out into the freedom of a whole new world, who could show me things I had never seen before. And my eyes were just beginning to open.

After a while, someone put up the money for my bond. It was my father. His generosity didn't draw me any closer to him, but I was thankful to be out. As long as I behaved myself, things would be fine. But they weren't.

Six months later, I was picked up on a drug indictment they had on me in Fluvanna County. Because of the amount and type of dealing I was doing, this was a very serious offense. With all the back time I would have to serve because of parole violations, I would be in prison for a long, long time.

Just how long, I didn't know.

A Spiritual Force

In many ways, all throughout my life, I had been a self-sufficient man. I was a fighter, a survivor. Nothing I ever did or ever knew prepared me for the losing battle I would face against drugs.

But losing was something I had to do in order to find out what winning was all about. Persistence and endurance would not win this battle. Cleverness and a strong work ethic were no match for the force that would control my life, driving me to hate everything I should love, making me despise life itself. As I discovered, this was far more than a physical or "psychological" addiction.

A man can be in jail for fifteen years, with no trace of drugs in his body. Yet by simply thinking about crack, he will feel the aftereffects. Fifteen years can go by without him touching the drug, and the day he gets out he goes right back to it.

He knows that the drug has controlled and destroyed his life, that it has taken his wife and family and made him a bum. But because he doesn't have any spiritual foundation to fight against it, he goes right back to it. It is the work of a controlling spirit in that man's life, and until he can submit to the God who can deliver him from it, he will never get away from it.

In Narcotics Anonymous and Alcoholics Anonymous, you learn to say, "Hello, my name is _____. I'm an alcoholic." Even if you're there for fifty years, those words never change. Your addiction remains the dominant force in your life. You're always "recovering," never completely free.

As good as those programs are, they can't deliver you from the drug. It takes a Savior to deliver you. That's why there are so many people still in bondage. What you're dealing with is a spirit, and until you battle it in the spirit, you can't win. That's what I came to find out.

SENT OUT

SAVING GRACE

CHAPTER FOUR

CAPTIVE
AUDIENCE

For the indictment in Fluvanna, I was sent to the regional jail in the nearby county of Orange. As they led me in, a huge man looked down on me from one of the blocks higher up and issued a challenge. I knew I would have to fight him. I didn't want to even think about what they would do to me if I didn't somehow "prove myself."

I didn't wait for him to come to me; I sought him out. When I entered the dorm block, he approached me, and the fight was on. Even though I gained a certain type of respect from the other guys for not backing down to the prison bully, it bothered me afterward that I had chosen to resort to violence. I was only beginning to understand about the peaceful character of Jesus. Somehow, my actions had seemed justified.

The truth was that I was still operating in the old patterns. In the chaplain's office, I had only gone through the ritual of becoming a Christian. I was interested, but not convinced. I had "prayed the prayer," but it wasn't from my heart.

Fix It

There were two young white brothers— they looked about 21 years old—who came in right after I did, apparently on cocaine charges. I was curious because they would read the Bible every day, so I approached them and asked them about their belief. They not only shared with me, but for some reason I couldn't understand, they began to read the Bible to me every night. I had been on drugs for so long it was hard for me to read. Now, I was just like a kid sitting before a teacher. If there was a God, I was ready to listen.

Years before, even when I had been drinking and on drugs, something about the Bible had drawn me. Something in there had life. I could feel it, but I couldn't explain it to you. I would be lying in bed at night and I'd turn to Joyce and say, "Read the Bible." She couldn't really make sense of that. She knew people who went to church, and my life sure didn't match up to theirs, but she read it anyway. It brought peace into my life, but I didn't know why exactly. Here in jail, awaiting my sentencing hearing, I would finally understand.

One day while I was sitting on my bunk, I remembered every time somebody had tried to tell me about Jesus. After what seemed like about half an hour, I got down on my knees, and I prayed. It wasn't eloquent. But it was real. It was from my heart.

"God, here's my life," I said. "Fix it. If you can fix this mess, I will serve you for the rest of my life."

This time, I wanted more than a way out of my problems. I was determined to change.

The response was immediate. All of a sudden I felt as if someone had dropped a 500-pound weight on me, pushing me to the floor. I was trembling, shaking all over. But I was not afraid. I knew—this time for sure—that there was a God out there.

Turnings

Even though I had an incredible encounter

with God, my focus wasn't completely on him. I was thinking of Joyce. I was trying to figure out how I could help her understand everything that had happened to me.

I knew I had to serve a lot of time, but all I wanted was an opportunity to be able to go back and talk to Joyce. I wanted to tell her that I loved her and wanted to marry her and spend the rest of my life with her. And I just prayed that somehow, even if she rejected me, I could be honest about what God had been doing in my life.

I knew I didn't deserve Joyce, but I loved her with all of my heart. Even when I was at my worst, whenever I had come and been open with her in the past, even then—I could see it clearly now—she was my best friend. I could tell Joyce something, and she would listen to me patiently and with a very kind heart. I prayed for her faithfully every night. I prayed she would give me one more chance.

After twenty-three days, I was still in jail, and there seemed no hope of getting out. I could not see Joyce, and there was nothing I could do about it. If I couldn't see her, I was sure I would lose her. I was stuck here while everything I loved was just slipping away.

I have lost everything. Just like I lost my mother, just like I lost my father, just like I lost my family. I have lost Joyce too. I have lost everything.

Angry and hurt, I reaccepted that "old man"—the attitude of the person I used to be. And I turned.

I cursed God with every ungodly name I could think of. All the bitterness in my heart poured out of my mouth. Everybody in the block stopped what they were doing and stared at me. In my mind this "God" I had just surrendered my life to was no better than my father. He had abandoned me. He had pushed me away like some unwanted stray.

"You're not God!" I yelled.

As soon as the words were out of my mouth, the prison officer walked through the door and said, "Washington, get all your stuff. Your bond came through."

I was stunned. Immediately I fell to my knees. "God forgive me," I cried out. It was as if God had been waiting for me all this time. Now he had his chance. Now he had my attention.

A presence came into that cell block so powerfully you could feel it. I looked around me. All the other men in the block were on their knees too! One was the guy I had fought when I first came there. Another was someone who had tried to harm me for no apparent reason. There was a man from Cuba and one from Africa. And there were the two white brothers who had been sharing the Bible with me. I'll never forget the look one of them had in his eyes. It was a piercing look—like his gaze could go right through you. And he was smiling as he said, "Brother Washington, God is faithful to his promises."

Time Out

When I got home to Joyce, I had so much to tell her. Of course we had been talking on the phone every so often since I'd entered the regional jail, but she had heard so much from me over the years—so many promises, how I was going to do this and that—that at first what I was telling her was just another one of "those things." After a while, Joyce seemed willing to believe there had been a change in me. She, too, was desperate for a way out of our old life.

Joyce listened like she always had, but she wasn't ready to commit herself to God. She needed to see more. But this was a start, a good start as far as I was concerned. I had time to share with her the joy of God's presence in my life. I had a chance to pray with my family. Those days were the happiest of my life.

At the end of about two weeks, it was time for me to return to court. Though I was forgiven and cleansed of all my guilt on the inside, before the law of the land I was still a criminal. There were two sentencing hearings, one in Fluvanna, the other before Judge Swett in Charlottesville. When it was all over, they had sentenced me to seventeen years, to run concurrently. At the very least, I would probably serve seven to ten years of that time. I accepted what was before me with a certain sadness, but also with great peace. Now, because of my new relationship with God, I had a purpose for living, wherever I had to live. I went back to the Orange Regional jail. I wasn't happy to be leaving my family, but I was confident that God would never leave me.

Solitary Refinement

Not long after I got back, a prison officer

came to our block in the middle of the night. He needed to speak to the two white brothers who had been sharing the Bible with me.

"Pack your bags," he told them. "It's time to go."

When I heard those words, my heart broke. I stood there looking at them with tears running down my face. Crying is not "good" to do in prison, but it was something I couldn't control. They had been my connection to this new life I was finding out about, and now they were gone.

The following day, I went to the prison chaplain's office broken and crying. These two men had left. How could I understand the Bible on my own? Reaching up to his shelf, he pulled down a Living Bible and handed it to me. This would be my next tutor.

I was lying in the bunk at two o'clock in the morning, reading my new Bible, when the raid began. Without warning, several officers and guards quickly snatched me out of the top bunk and pushed me down to the floor. Lifting my hands above my head, they rushed me out of the block. Any slowness on their part in taking a prisoner could easily result in a riot.

Confused and shaken, I asked them over

and over, "What have I done? What have I done?" They claimed I had been trying to start a riot. That had no truth to it at all. I didn't know what they were talking about. I was the most peaceful man in the whole block. In fact, I was even fearful because I had been away a month and had just gotten back. Somehow they had gotten me mixed up with somebody else.

They locked me in solitary confinement for ten days. I couldn't call Joyce or get in touch with her. It was driving me crazy not to be able to find out how she was doing.

But there in the "lock down" I had the opportunity of a lifetime. From the minute I landed there, I began to pray like never before. God and I had long conversations, usually about six hours each day. At night when I went to sleep, I held my new Bible close to me, just like a baby holding a teddy bear.

In the morning, when I woke, I sensed his presence with me, and I'd say, "Good morning, Father." The Bible became so alive to me. I cried out to God in prayer, and he spoke to me through his Word. This wasn't just a book of helpful sayings; it was life-giving truth for me.

After ten days the prison officers came to

my cell. "We made a mistake," they said. "It wasn't you."

That may have been their mistake, but it wasn't God's. It was a time that he had held especially for me. He took away my "false god"—the two white brothers that I had met—and he revealed himself. No more did I have to worry about people coming in and leaving. When I first came into the jail, I was so desperate to learn about God and be close to him that when someone would even mention the name "God," I would cling to them, regardless of their spiritual background. Now God was showing me, "It's not about men. It's about me and you—a personal relationship."

Spreading the Fire

The two white brothers who had been reading the Bible to me had started a prayer group even before I had been released on bond. About half of the guys in the cell block—including Muslims, those without any certain beliefs, and even men who had no respect for the law—would gather together to hold hands and pray. It wasn't your typical "prayer meeting," but we all understood two things—we needed help, and we wanted to know God better.

Even though that prayer time was good, I knew in my spirit that it could be more. When I went back to the cell block, it was up to me to start the prayer group again. At first, there were just two of us—me and the guy I had fought when I first came into the jail. In time, we grew to a group of thirty. We were getting together every night, and the prayer had a "trickle-down" effect throughout the whole facility. This time the guys were recognizing who God was, and we prayed in Jesus' name. God was with us in those times of prayer.

Even though I had been having long, private conversations with God, I was clueless how to pray in a group like that. I was just learning how to pray myself. I prayed for all of the guys there, just as I had done when I was alone with the Lord, but now I prayed those words out loud. I was "not ashamed of the gospel of Jesus Christ, because it is the power of God unto salvation for those who believe."

And I believed it.

Family Matters

The longer I stayed in jail, the more I understood that "this God thing" was real. I watched very evil men that I had grown up with change right before my eyes. A lot of my family was selling drugs, and many of them showed up in jail sooner or later. I saw my cousins change for the better. The difference in their lives was dramatic, and I knew God had done it.

But my main concern was even closer to home. I wanted to see Joyce know this God too. I kept sending Christians over to the house to befriend her, even though she was annoyed when all these strangers started showing up at her door. I also started a Bible study with her over the phone. She'd never been to church herself, and she was still very skeptical, but she went along with it.

After a while, I was transferred to the Charlottesville-Albemarle Joint Security Complex to serve some back time there. That's when I think Joyce's encounter with God began. My cousin Clifford was a caring Christian man. I had lied to him to get money when I was on drugs, but Clifford was always a good example and used to talk to me all the time about God. Now that I was in jail, Clifford started talking to Joyce about God too.

In the evenings, Joyce would visit Clifford and Delphine's house. Week after week Joyce promised she'd go to church with them, but when Sunday morning came around she always had an excuse. As they spoke to her about a God whose love never failed, she knew she needed and wanted that kind of love. She knew her own life was hopeless, and she felt an emptiness that somehow she knew God could fill.

Finally—as she told me later—one Sunday morning she went to church. When the minister invited those who wanted to ask Christ into their hearts to come to the front, Joyce got out of her seat and walked forward.

It was a step of faith going to that altar. She didn't know what was going to happen. All of it was new to her. But everything she had been hearing was something she needed in her life. When she got there, someone had her repeat a prayer of confession and commitment.

Just like my time in the chaplain's office repeating a similar prayer, it was a beginning. But there was so much more to come.

Jailhouse Bliss

It was about a year into my sentence when Joyce first put her trust in God. Now, the prayers over the telephone began to get real. We talked about important issues and spiritual things. And one of the most important things on my heart was to ask Joyce to be my wife.

I prayed and prayed about that for a long time, and finally I got the nerve to ask her over the phone. But before I asked her to marry me, I had to ask her forgiveness.

"I know I haven't been a faithful man to you," I confessed to her. "I haven't been a good provider for you and the kids, but I'm asking for another chance. Something has happened to me this time. It's not the same William who came in these doors that's going to be coming out."

She had heard promises like this before, and every time they were broken.

"I believe that in order to honor God in our relationship, one of the things we need to do, and I want to do, is get married. I want to marry you. I want to spend the rest of my life with you. I love you. Will you come over here and marry me while I'm in jail?"

She wouldn't give me an answer right away, and I couldn't blame her. I was asking her to be faithful to someone who had not been faithful to her. It would take some time for her to think it over.

I knew that what I had presented was not just from my own heart. God had put it there. I was dead serious about my commitment this time. If I couldn't live a productive life when I got out of jail, I didn't want to get out.

About a week later, I was on the phone again with Joyce. We talked once more about our future, and she explained her concerns because I hadn't lived up to my past promises. But I believe she was hearing something different this time. Finally, she gave me her decision.

"Yes," she said, and I found myself smiling, "I'll come over and marry you."

But there was one other obstacle. The chaplain at the jail refused to marry inmates. He had seen too many of these "marriages" end before they had a chance to begin. But he sensed something different with Joyce and me. He agreed to marry us if Joyce and I were willing to go through premarital counseling together. We were. Once a week for the next eight weeks, the two of us met in his office as he tried to explain to us what a real marriage was all about.

I had never really understood what a husband was supposed to be like. In fact, there were a lot of things I didn't understand about family life. But those counseling sessions really helped me. Through that chaplain, God's hand was at work in my life. He laid a good foundation that would last for years to come.

Finally, a few weeks after Christmas in the winter of 1992, Joyce and I were married in the Charlottesville-Albemarle Joint Security Complex. Right after the ceremony, Joyce headed back home. We were married, but for now, we would have to be apart.

Hope for New Life

About two months later, I heard of a program called New Life for Youth. From what I understood, it was a place where people who had come out of a drug background could learn how to grow up in God.

One day I was talking with Joyce on the phone about it. "I just believe God is going to do something for us, that he's going to bring us together," I told her. "I don't know how he's going to do it, but I believe we have made the right step in getting married. God is pleased, and I feel like some favor is going to come from this."

I went to the chaplain and told him I wanted to go to New Life. I was hopeful, but realistic. "I've got seventeen years," I reminded him, "and when the judge gave me that, he was being lenient. It should have been more than that."

"Well," the chaplain said simply, "let's go back before the judge and see what happens."

The first place I had to appear was Fluvanna. When I got up before the bench, the first thing the judge did was make a joke about Christianity. I said to myself, *Well, so much for this one.* When it came time for his decision, though, the Fluvanna judge said, "I'm not going to make a ruling in this case. I'm going to send you to Charlottesville to the circuit court judge again." That meant I would be before the presiding judge there, Judge Swett.

In Charlottesville, the prosecutor recounted my prior criminal history, providing a detailed list of my crimes and failures. Then it was my turn to speak.

"Your Honor," I began, "the things the prosecutor told you are very much true, and there are some others he doesn't know about. But, sir, I really want this chance. If you give me this opportunity, I know it will change my life."

Judge Swett pulled his glasses down to the end of his nose and just stared at me. For what seemed like several minutes he didn't say a word. Steadily meeting his gaze, I wondered, *What in the world is this man thinking about?*

After a time, he sat back in his chair. Still, there was no response. I stood there, waiting and hoping. Finally he broke the silence.

"Is there anything else you want to say?"

"No, your Honor."

"Young man," the judge addressed me, "I'm going to grant you your wish. I'm going to give you the opportunity to go through this program. But I'm going to put some tight guidelines around you."

When the judge was finished, I had six years of probation, three years of that with urine screening, followed by another three years of unsupervised probation if I did well for the first three. If I failed to do right, I had an automatic seventeen years waiting for me in jail. On top of that, after I finished the New Life program, I had to get a job and pay restitution.

They were high standards, but I knew that God could get me through. For now, he had given me an unbelievable opportunity to go to New Life for Youth, and I would make the most of every single day.

A Solid Foundation

My life was a wreck when I came to God: I had nothing. I had built it upon hurt, pain, and rejection, and they were still at the core. God had to begin with me from the ground up, from the inside out.

I knew I had nothing to offer God and everything to receive from him. That was a good place to start.

At first, I depended on men, on those whom God sent my way. We need godly relationships to keep us strong. We need people who can challenge us when our actions don't match up with our words. But ultimately, our faith cannot be built upon that foundation. Men can shift just like the sand.

I am thankful to know today that my relationship with God wasn't built upon men. My relationship with God was built as I spent time with him in prayer and in reading the Bible. Because of my relationship with God I can sing and dance and pray and study his Word for hours and it often seems like minutes. I long for the presence of God to grow in my life, to be real in my actions and in my words.

When I am alone with God, worshiping him, there is nowhere else I want to be. It is the best way I know to bring encouragement and freedom and confidence into my life.

CHAPTER FIVE
NEW LIFE

As the probation officer and I drove onto the grounds at New Life for Youth, I knew in my heart that I was in the right place. Beyond me I could see men gathered in front of a huge, white house, working on the facility, painting, and mowing the grass.

But what really got my attention was the sign at the entrance. Underneath the name was a verse of Scripture, 2 Corinthians 5:17, the same one that I had held on to during my time in the cell: "Therefore, if anyone is in Christ, he is a new creation; old things have passed away; behold, all things have become new." I saw it as a confirmation that God had sent me here. More than anything, at twenty-seven years old, I wanted those words to be true in my own life.

A Father's Love

Each morning I would get up early to

spend time with God. There was nothing else I wanted to do more than have a relationship with him. I was experiencing a father that I never had before. As a child I remembered there were moments when I didn't want to be with anyone else but my father. With God, that was every day. I had a lot of questions, but the Scriptures I read answered them almost as quickly as they came up.

I was learning to love God like I wanted to love my father. I wanted to serve God like God had served me by giving me an opportunity to start my life all over again.

For the first time in my life, I was real in my relationship with God. I lived by and honored everything I read in the Bible. The things I couldn't do on my own, God helped me to do. He showed me how through his Word.

The most important thing in my life was my family—Joyce and my kids—but I had never been a husband before, had never been a father before. The example I had been given in my own life was wrong. The results of my own life gave plenty of evidence for that. But the Bible showed me how to be a father and husband—in very practical ways—and I was so excited to find out. I was learning things I never knew before. What I read brought understanding. My obedience to it brought change.

I now understood that God was my heavenly father. He would be all of the father I ever needed—a perfect father—and yet I had failed him over and over again. In spite of that, God still loved me. He hadn't rejected me. He still wanted me to be his son.

I had read in God's Word about the time Jesus told the hypocrites to stop looking for the sin in others when they had plenty of their own. "Why do you look for the speck of sawdust in your brother's eye," he asked them, "but don't consider the beam that is in your own eye?"

I knew that my own father had been wrong. He had hurt me deeply, but that did not let me off the hook. I had a problem with unforgiveness, and I had to own it.

I also knew from reading the Bible that unless I forgave my father, I couldn't be forgiven. That unforgiveness, that bitterness, would be like an anchor holding me back. If I held on to the past, I wouldn't be able to move forward.

Over and over God continued to affirm his

love for me as a father. The more I understood that, the softer my heart became.
Because God had forgiven me so much, I was
able to begin to forgive my own father for
what he had done. It was another step, another beginning. There would be other times
when I would need to come to God with
memories from my past and a need to forgive.
But each time, God removed the hurt and
pain and replaced it with his love.

Home Safe

There was another wound my father gave
me that I had to deal with. I had been at New
Life for about three months when the bullet
that was still in my foot started causing a lot
of problems. For years it had never bothered
me that much. Now my foot was aching and
swollen. I tried to walk on the side of it to
ease the pain, but this was only a temporary
solution. It soon became obvious I had to
have an operation. Arrangements were made
to give me a six-month leave of absence, and
before I knew it, I was on my way home.

This was the second time the wound in my
foot had brought me to Charlottesville. The
first time, I was running away from my fami-

ly—this time, I was running to it. And, although I didn't know it at first, I was going home to save my family. The operation went well. The surgery mostly affected the arch of my foot. I still had several weeks of recovery, but regardless, I was on leave for a full six months.

I had come back at the perfect time. Joyce really needed someone to walk this new Christian life alongside her. She was already sliding back into her old lifestyle. If God had not brought me home when he did, I don't think I would have had a family waiting for me.

Just as God showed me how to love my father, he gave me a love for Joyce that was beyond me. I loved her so much that there was nothing she could do to push me away from her. There was no type of sin she could have committed that would have stopped me from loving her. And she finally saw that.

One night I overheard her talking on the telephone. "His life has been changed," she said to her friend. "He actually lives by the things he talks about."

It was important for her to see the changes God was working in my life, but she couldn't have a relationship with God just by watching me. "I really don't understand," she would tell me.

One day, though, God captured her heart. In tears, she came to me and confessed everything she had done while I was gone. It turned into a time of repentance for both of us, and it was a time of challenges. But it was the first step in the growth of our marriage.

After that, trust and respect for her rose up within me. Before, we had always been suspicious of each other, but God removed that completely. Now we had a marriage based on the truth of God's Word, and we were loving each other for the very first time.

Family

Once Joyce and I were on a good foundation with our marriage, you could see the effects on our entire family. Our four children were still young. Gregory was ten; Shanta, six; Waverly, four; and Marquis, only two. Even though they had been so little when I was on drugs, I knew they had felt the effects. I would have told someone back then that I had a relationship with my children, but it wouldn't have been the truth. That relationship was based on what I learned about fatherhood from my own father. Now I was learning from my perfect, heavenly Father.

As I began to spend a lot of time with the kids—talking with them, building confidence in them, playing with them—Joyce and I watched our children embrace God in a way that was amazing. We could see God's hand upon them, and we loved to listen to their simple, genuine prayers.

It was good that our marriage and our family were strong and growing, but that wasn't enough. There was more that we wanted to do than just serve each other and our children.

"Lord," we asked simply, "what do you want us to do?"

The answer was to start right where we were.

Beyond Our Walls

Joyce and I wanted to represent the whole truth of who God is and what he can do, but there were some challenges. Everyone in the neighborhood knew about our old lifestyle and its deception. To suddenly go from that kind of life to telling everyone that we were

Christians made some people think we were hypocrites. So now you're supposed to be holy? Who are you kidding?

Our job was to live the truth before them, and over the next three or four months, people saw the difference. They knew where we had been and what we had done, but they could see our lives changing in ways they knew were real.

Especially since there was such little support in our neighborhood, we knew it was important for our family to have close ties with other Christians. The only church I had really known—Christ Community Church—was no longer meeting at the school where I had first found them. They had a building of their own now, and by the incredible grace of God, it was right in the middle of our neighborhood!

The people who lived near us were mostly African American, and Christ Community was predominantly a white, middle-class church. At first it was a challenge for me to go there. I had always believed all white people were just as hard and cold as my grandfather had been.

But over the years God had been breaking

down that prejudice. Many of the people who had spoken to me about the Lord were lighter skinned. And wasn't it two white brothers who shared the Bible every night with me when I was in the regional jail? Obviously, I had been wrong. But it would take me a while longer to trust.

In spite of my reluctance, these people kept reaching out to me. John Manzano, the pastor who had come to the jail, found some much-needed work for me at the church. My foot was recovering nicely, and because the incision had been in the arch, I could walk pretty well without putting direct pressure on it. In addition to a few basic cleanup duties, he had me mow the church's four-acre lawn with a twenty-two-inch lawnmower he purchased. By the time I finished the last part, the first part was ready to be mowed again!

John really was looking for a way to keep me busy with a full-time job. He wanted to keep me around and see how serious I was about providing for my family. Every day I showed up for work and did what I was supposed to do. I honored God, John, and the job.

With all the kindness I received from the

members of this church, it became more difficult to hold the hard line on my prejudice
against "white people." They supported us,
they encouraged us, and they challenged us to
live godly lives. I had never received that kind
of support before. These people were becoming like family to me, and no one was more
surprised than I was.

Especially important were the Sunday services our family attended faithfully each week.
I took in the Word of God like a thirsty man
needing a long, cold drink of water. And what
I received, I turned around and gave to those
in the neighborhood, because they needed it
as much as I did.

Home Group

One way we gave back to the neighborhood was by starting a home group. Joyce
and I got together a few people who met
faithfully every Monday night to pray, to
worship God, and to study the Bible. There
would be anywhere from five to eleven people
who came to our home, each of them very
open to the work of God in their own lives.
And the Lord began to deliver them too.

For about half an hour, we read from the

Bible and I explained what I knew, what I had been learning. But most of our time was spent in prayer and worship. Sometimes the meetings would last three or four hours. There were so many needs, so much that needed to be made right. We were learning who God is and what he can do, and as we prayed, we believed he would answer.

Spiritually, Joyce and I were like two babies, and God was just feeding us. I believe that's true for most new Christians. God kind of babysits you and spoils you. That's what was happening for us. Every prayer we prayed was answered according to what was best for us—according to God's will. We recorded it all in a book, an amazing account of God's faithfulness to us.

Prayer was a vital part of what we did, but it wasn't all of it. Through these conversations with God and growing in our understanding of his Word, we extended to our neighbors the same hands we raised to God in prayer.

We didn't have much ourselves, but then, everyone in our neighborhood was needy. If we had an extra meal and someone was in need, we shared it. We helped provide groceries and other financial support. Sometimes we even gave money set aside for our own rent. That made it even tighter for us, but God always provided.

All during these days, God's grace was so evident that we felt carried through our many challenges. It was not about us. It was about God's people. It was about people who had never met him, who had never known this joy we had. Those were the people we really cared about. We just wanted them to have the same peace and joy we now had in our lives. And we believed they could have it if they really wanted to.

Fall Back

More than ever before, my heart turned toward Joyce and the kids. Because I knew it was God's plan for every husband to provide for his family, I was determined to do whatever it took to do so. After my foot was completely healed, I would have to go back to New Life. In the meantime, I was going to make the most of every opportunity to bless my family.

Besides mowing the grass at Christ Community, I took on lots of extra work—

anything I could find that would help pay the bills. At night, people would bring me their cars to work on. I still had a reputation as a top-notch detailer, and I never lacked for work. God provided the opportunities, and he gave me the grace to put forth the effort.

After six months, my recovery from the foot surgery was complete. In another week or so I would be going back to New Life. I had grown so much in my walk with the Lord, and I was thankful to be able to share my testimony with so many people. But there was one group I hadn't seen yet—my extended family back in the country—and I was set on paying them a visit before I left.

Over and over Joyce had warned me not to go back to my family. She had become a true helpmeet to me during these last months, and she knew the weaknesses I had. I still longed to be accepted by them, though, and that clouded my judgment.

Ignoring everything she had said, I got a ride back to the country. And as soon as I got there, I realized how right she had been. I knew I had crossed a line that I shouldn't have crossed.

I was reminded of what I had read in the

Bible, the command to be separated from the things we used to do and from companions that would lead us back into those old ways. I went right back in the middle of those people for a good reason: to share with them what God had done for me, to let them know there was a way out of the lifestyle they were living. But it was not my time to do that.

Before I knew it, I was back into everything that God had delivered me from. Drugs. Smoking. Drinking. I was headed down the same path I had come from. Back in town, I was teaching other people how to live by the Word of God, but I didn't have the wisdom to keep myself out of trouble.

"You shouldn't be here," my cousin told me. "Come on, I'll take you home." He put me in the truck and started driving back to Charlottesville.

I was a broken man during that ride. I felt like nothing. As soon as I walked in the door, I confessed to my wife what had happened. I also called John, my pastor, and confessed it to him. There were still a few days before I was scheduled to return to New Life, but I sensed God was telling me to go back right away. I needed something more, and it couldn't wait.

New Sight

Almost as soon as I returned to New Life, I realized something was different, but I couldn't quite put my finger on it. It seemed like the fire that all of the residents once had for the Lord was gone. Things seemed dead. Looking back, I now think they must have grown stagnant in their spiritual walk. They hadn't stepped up to the next level, but by being at home and becoming a leader in the community, I had.

As a result, I began to grow as a leader at New Life too. I exercised the gifts that God had given me—gifts that had remained quiet during the first months I had stayed there.

Of course, I still had spiritual needs that needed attention, areas where I needed to grow stronger. First, God spoke to me about his forgiveness. Though I had fallen back into my old ways, he let me know he forgave me. He loved me and wanted to be my father. After that finally sank in—that God really did love me—I had a joy that no one could ever take away. He also spoke to me clearly that right now I needed to stay away from my natural family. He told me to provide for my own family, and to let the way I lived my life be the evidence of change that others could see.

God was somehow taking my weakness and my sin and using it again for his glory. But I knew that this was not just another opportunity for me. This was a matter of life and death. If I went back to the world, I was a dead man. This was my last chance. Like Peter once said to Jesus, "Lord, to whom shall we go? You have the words of eternal life." Later on—especially during times when I wanted to give up—God would bring to mind these same words to encourage me.

After a month there, the director of the program called me in to his office one day. "I've been checking up on what you were doing while you were out," he said. He had opened my files from the parole officer, had listened to different people, and had even called my pastor.

"William," he said, "what we offer here, you've already accomplished. There's no reason you should be staying here. You've completed the program."

I had been a resident there for a little more than five months out of a standard eighteen-month program, but I was finished. God had taken me where he wanted me to be. I went home again to my wife, my family, and the community we were serving.

I had a lifetime to live now, and I was free.

Waiting in Order

Each time in my life that God has wanted to prepare me for something, he has brought me close to him. Then, when my relationship with God has grown to the point where I am ready for the next challenge, he releases me into it.

My time at New Life was to prepare me to serve my wife, my family, and then—together—our community. That is the order God has for his people.

I see so many people today who want to help others spiritually, but they themselves haven't learned how to walk. They take care of others, but they don't know how to take care of themselves.

This is what happened to me. I knew the command of God to go out into the world and tell others, and I felt a strong desire to help those around me, but I had no one to tell me that there were steps to take in between. My own foundation was very thin.

Waiting is a time of growth and learning. It is time well spent, and there is no other kind of time that can take its place. In waiting, we learn to trust, and trust is the basis of every true friendship, especially friendship with God.

I thank God that he makes us wait, that he helps us to build on a strong foundation before the storm comes, that he doesn't turn us out into the next battle before we're ready.

Then, by his grace, our challenges become victories.

CHAPTER SIX

TOUGH GOING

I had seen how quickly and easily I could slip back into my old lifestyle and old way of thinking. I had to have a plan, so I started seeking out people to whom I could be accountable, people who would help hold me responsible to my commitments to God, to my family, and to myself.

For starters, I became part of a men's group at Christ Community. We met every Monday at five o'clock in the afternoon. Two hours later, the prayer group Joyce and I started would meet at our home. Once a week I met with one of the pastors in our church who helped me learn how to read and understand the Bible, and every month I got together with John to talk about how to apply what I was learning—how to be faithful to my wife, how to raise my children well, to see that they got a good education and were taught how to follow God in their lives. On top of that, Joyce

117

and I had prayer together as a couple and with our children. I had a lot of accountability in my life, and I doubt I could have kept going without it.

Character Witnesses

What I found in these meetings were men who lived out the Scriptures, whose lives had order and structure. In the Monday afternoon men's group, we started supporting each other, holding each other responsible to talk about our weaknesses. And we didn't stop with the easy questions.

Of course, I had also gone back to mowing the lawn at church, and that meant more time around the leadership there. I gained so much from those men. Without even realizing it, I was learning how to live honestly and rightly. I never asked anyone to sit down and explain it to me. I just watched how they functioned, how they interacted with each other, even in intense times. That was good for me to see. I needed walking examples.

John shared with me what it took to be a caring husband, and I was amazed that he actually did what he said. Since I'd seen so much hypocrisy in my life, I was always skeptical. But with John, you could tell that what he was saying was true, and he was living it. That's something I had been wanting.

You see, even though I was a Christian, I wasn't complete. I still had a lot of bad patterns and wrong habits. I know those men saw a lot of my weaknesses, but they still loved me. The truth doesn't come easily for a man who's lived a lie all his life. I had to understand the truth and have it explained to me day by day. To know the truth, you've got to want the truth.

I knew Jesus said, "I am the Way, the Truth, and the Life," but what was the truth for me when my whole life had been a lie? Since the age of fourteen I had been doing just about anything to survive. As a child, I never had an example at home that said, "Live right. Live truthfully."

The only thing I had brought from home was the ability to work hard. I was putting that into practice on the grounds at Christ Community Church, but I was learning something more. I learned to take that persistence and start applying it to the weaknesses in my life. When I'd slip and fall, I didn't stay down there. I kept getting back up. When people criticized me harshly, I still kept getting back up. Some of the things they said were true! I needed to hear them.

The people around me could only give me so much. I had to work out the details of this new life for myself. I had to be changed. The support and accountability were essential for me, but I was the one responsible for walking it out.

Walking It Out

As hard as it was, I had to deal with the consequences of every single thing I had done during my days of drinking and being on drugs—every last one of them. I had fines and court-ordered restitution payments, and there was a stack of unpaid bills. But they were the smaller issues. The deeper ones were harder: the ways I had neglected my wife and caused her pain; the people that I had hurt when I was selling drugs; the rejection of my father; the emptiness I still felt from the loss of my mother. Some of these issues I just couldn't handle; I didn't have the power or the strength. Without this new understanding I had received through reading God's Word and putting it into practice, I never would have made it. Because of my previous lifestyle, I was now heavily in debt. That by itself could have been overwhelming, but I just knew that God would provide a way for us, just as he had been doing.

At first, my wife and I walked everywhere we went. We couldn't even afford a taxi cab. It was sometimes a two-mile walk just to get groceries. That was the time of our humility.

A couple of months after I returned from New Life, John told me I needed to find a job that would support my family. The church couldn't do any more than they were already doing.

Thankfully, I did find a job working at an auto body shop about a half an hour by car from our house. The problem was, I didn't have a driver's license and I didn't have a car. And in order to get a license, I would first have to pay all my old traffic violations— about fourteen hundred dollars. By working side jobs, after a while I managed to put that much money aside. I cleared that debt completely. What a relief. The Friday before I was to start my new job, my sister drove me to get my license.

"I'm sorry, Mr. Washington," the clerk surprised me by saying, "but you still have some unpaid fines."

"That's impossible," I said. "I paid every one of them."

"Not according to what's on my records," she replied, looking back at her computer screen.

I couldn't believe it. The unpaid fines came to about three hundred dollars, but it may as well have been three hundred thousand dollars. I didn't have anything left, and without a license, I wasn't going to have a job on Monday.

It seemed there was nothing more I could say or do, so I turned to walk away. Then something made me stop. Turning around, I faced the clerk again.

"I really need this job to take care of my family."

"I'm sorry. I can't help you."

Slowly, my sister and I walked out of the building. What was I going to do? After all this work, the door seemed to be shut just as firmly as before.

"Mr. Washington!"

I turned to see the clerk running out into the parking lot.

"Mr. Washington, here's what I can do. I'm going to give you a temporary license. That will give me some time to check on these records. If everything is fine, then I can issue your regular driver's license."

Wow! Thankfully, a few minutes before, I had not gotten angry and gone back into my old way of handling things. I was learning how to be humble in the face of opposition. Now that was something new.

On top of all that, right after I received my license, a lady in our church allowed us to purchase a car from her with no money down and low payments.

I was ready to get to work.

Stepping Up, Stepping Down

When I had first applied for the job at the auto body shop, the boss, Mr. Hall, was excited about my experience as a detailer. Unfortunately, there was not enough of that type of work then to make a full-time job. He did need someone to help with janitorial work, though. I was used to making a lot more money working on cars than what I would be paid, but I saw this as an opportunity to prove myself.

One of the first days I was there, the joke of the day for the guys in the shop had something to do with where African Americans lived—and they didn't exactly use the phrase "African Americans." When I came in for work, one or two of the guys would take a big pile of trash and throw it out on the floor in front of me. I would nod, smile, and pick up the trash.

Lunch time was another challenge. Everyone would congregate together to laugh and talk. I chose to spend my time apart, reading the Bible. Every now and then they would throw an old rag or can in my direction, but I chose not to react. It really didn't have much to do with the color of my skin. They just liked to tease that way. They were testing me.

All I did was work hard. I cleaned the toilets like they had never been cleaned before. I kept the shop floor neat and shining. Whatever I was asked to do, I worked at it with all my energy. I used my time wisely. When break time was up, I was back on the job.

Mr. Hall and his son, Brent, were two of the answers to the calling on my life. All three of us had the same zeal for work. Mr. Hall had started at the bottom with almost nothing and had built a successful business. He was an example to me of hard work and endurance.

Watching and working for Mr. Hall, I realized that I didn't have to be in bondage to my upbringing or my past life. Mr. Hall was a man of patience and kindness. He took time to make sure I understood what he needed me to do. I had never received that kind of treatment from my father. In many ways, I was getting a new family in the Halls, and I prayed faithfully for them.

Pocket Change

About this time, Joyce and I made a decision to get off Aid to Dependent Children, money we received through our local Social Services Department to help pay for basic needs like food and clothing. That program had helped a lot of people, but for me it had become a sort of bondage. I didn't know where the extra money was going to come from, but inside I knew that I needed to be the one providing for my family. I had grown up with that knowledge, and everything I read in the Bible confirmed it. This decision was a step of faith for us, but we wanted to make it on our own. That's when things became really difficult.

I had a good job, and I was working about sixty hours a week, but I was still responsible for a huge amount of court-ordered payments. Every week 65 percent of my paycheck went to child support, another 15 percent went to restitution. That left me with a take home of fifty-three dollars a week, sometimes less. After I filled up the car with gas and took care of a few basic things, I had enough money to put food on the table for a day, maybe two.

Everything in me and everyone around me was saying, "You're not going to make it." Drug dealers I used to work with would come by and try to get me to go back. They had plenty of money all the time, and I could barely provide our daily needs.

What they said made a lot of sense. Wasn't I supposed to be supporting my family? Was I going to work hard for the rest of my life and still be struggling to meet my most basic needs?

Yet there was something in me—that hope in me—that kept reassuring me, *You're gonna*

make it. You're gonna make it. When everything was saying, "It's over. Your life is
worthless," the Word of God was saying,
"You can overcome." And that's what I
believed in.

New Addiction

When I woke up each morning I knew God
was with me. My first hour or more was
spent in worship and prayer and reading my
Bible. I got to work early in the morning and
came back around supper time. After dinner,
people would often stop by and ask me if I
could detail their car. I might not get to bed
until midnight. The next day I'd get up and
do it all over again. With that kind of schedule, each day I needed strength.

My prayers often started out with a lot of
frustration from the things I was dealing with
every day. But as I spent time with my heavenly father, I realized that he was so much
bigger than anything I was facing. Before I
knew it, my frustrations would turn into worship. I might be upstairs for two hours just
singing and praising. Even though my
resources were limited and I didn't know
where I was going to get the next meal for my

family, I was having the best time of my life.

I knew I couldn't find what I needed in my wife. I couldn't find it in my friends. I couldn't find it in my pastors. They were trying to encourage me, but I could only find what I really needed in God.

As far as I was concerned, there was nothing that could take the place of that time each morning. I had to have it. I poured out the deepest parts of my heart: *Just give me strength. Help me go on. I am not going to be defeated. I'm not going back to those drugs.* I used to gaze at my kids and my wife, and just seeing them would motivate me. *I'm going to be there for Joyce. I am going to be a father to my kids.*

Every morning, the joy I found carried me through that day.

A Father's Visit

One day we got a phone call. It was the jail.

"Your father is here," the voice said. "He has served his time, but he's very ill. Can you come pick him up?"

All the frustration and anger that I had in my heart toward him came back. I didn't want to go get him. I remembered how he could be when he was drinking. But I found something deep within that I thought was no longer there: a love for my father. I decided to follow my heart.

"We'll come and get him," I said.

He had been in jail for a couple of days. They had picked him up off the street where he had been lying, very close to death. Now he was also going through alcohol withdrawal and experiencing delirium tremens—DTs as it's called. It sends your body into violent convulsions. You can see and hear things that aren't there. It can even be fatal. They had gotten medical attention for my father, of course, but it wasn't helping. He had plenty of other physical problems after years of living like he had.

When I first saw him I was reminded of the man who shot me when I was fourteen, the man I ran away from, the man I had seen beat my mother unconscious. They brought him out in a wheelchair, and I supported him to the car. We didn't have room at our apartment for him to sleep, so he was going to move in with my sister. The ride to her house was very quiet.

Either before or after work I would go and check on him, making sure he had enough food and the right medicines—whatever he needed. And we began praying for him. Within a few days, the DTs had run its course, but he was still a very sick man. His kidneys were not working well at all, and the same was true for his liver. After several weeks of watching him, I just couldn't believe that all the medicines were doing him any good—not that I'm against taking medicine for the right reasons—it's just that in my father's case, they seemed to be doing more harm than good. So we kept praying.

Eventually I saw my father's strength returning. We made sure he was eating right and doing the things he was supposed to. A couple of weeks later, after his health had improved, we invited him to church. He started attending church on a regular basis, and you could see it had an impact on his life. He began to see the difference between the way he had been living and the life he saw in my family.

One day my father and I were at my house, and I was talking to him about what God had done in my life, how I had been changed. I told him I had found my peace with God, and that God wanted to share that peace with him through our Savior, the Lord Jesus Christ. God was not foreign to my father. He knew.

"Do you want your life back?" I asked him.

"Yes," he told me.

I prayed with him, and he asked God to forgive him and bring direction into his life. As I started seeing a change in him, my heart began to open. I wanted my father back. I found in myself that son who longed to be with his father and love and respect him. Every chance I got, I wanted to spend time with him.

My father wanted that time also. He loved to stop by our house two or three times a week. We talked a lot, and we became very close—the best of friends. I really enjoyed having him around. He did a lot of things with the kids too. Not only was he becoming a father, he was becoming a grandfather.

Neighborhood Needs

Having my father around was a wonderful experience for us, and his growth was part of our growth as a family. We were continually amazed in the ways God provided. Even though the courts were taking almost all of my wages, with the extra income from car detailing I could still bring home the equivalent of a regular paycheck. Amazingly, everything was working out. The hard work and endurance still had to be there, but grace was also there—in abundance and beyond our resources. Somehow, some way, there was always enough money to meet our needs. It didn't make sense, but that's just what happened.

Of course, the needs in our neighborhood were just as great as ever, and we wanted to give to them in the same way we had been blessed.

In many ways, I guess you could say that Joyce and I became like a father and mother to that community. We took the kids to the county fair, listened to people's problems, and took time to help them. We didn't usually have extra money, but we always figured out a way to help people when they were in need. When I found out someone else's car was broken, I showed up with my toolbox and said, "Let's fix it." We shared what we had, and there was always enough.

Christ Community became more and more involved in our community, too—financially and in other ways—and we were a vehicle for that blessing. They provided Thanksgiving baskets for a lot of folks in the neighborhood. They had programs for the kids. Little by little, we saw this once-broken community begin to be transformed. Without the presence and love of God, it could never have happened at all.

A Car Story

Financially, each day continued to be a challenge. There was always something else that needed fixing or replacing. One day, the car stopped working, and I had no way to get to the body shop. I was sitting there with three dollars in my pocket, no food on the table, and I was about to lose my job. Despite all I was learning and experiencing about God firsthand, it still could have been so easy to go back to the old ways, the "easy" money.

My son Waverly was about six years old at the time. He was growing in faith right along with me. "Waverly," I said, "everything is going wrong. Would you pray?" I don't remember everything he prayed, but it touched my heart. I could hear him saying, "God bless my daddy. God bless my daddy."

At the end of the prayer we got a phone call. A woman we knew from church was on the line. "William," she said, "I just got a new car. I wonder if you could use my old one."

She sold us that car for one dollar. That left two dollars for gas to make it to work the next day. Just enough.

That's the hope we have—that God will always make a way.

Big surprises like getting a car didn't happen that often. Most of the stories from those days were quieter, less dramatic. We had what we needed for each day, and that was enough.

Even the car was a trial in its own way. For one thing, it didn't have a heater. Not only did I have to wrap up—worse than that, the windshield wouldn't defrost. When it was cold I would drive about thirty miles per hour, wiping the windshield with one hand and driving with the other. People got so frustrated with me! They would blow their horns and try to speed up to go around me, yelling, "Get off the road!"

Yes, my life still had plenty of challenges. Serving God didn't mean everything was going to be easy. But I knew one thing: He was taking care of me, and that was more than enough.

Back to Jail

Around the time I started the job at Hall's, the Lord gave me this direction for my life: "The same grace that I've given you, the same way that I've given you, go give it to others."

I loved the Lord so much, and people could sense that when I prayed. But I was still so new to this. I didn't have a lot of maturity in my life. Developing that would be a process, an ordered and directed process.

One day I got an invitation from a pastor to speak at a church. My own pastor knew I wasn't ready for that, and he had the boldness to tell me. I appreciated his honesty and his firmness, and I passed up the opportunity.

One place my pastor did let me go and preach was the jail. Because I had come out of that setting, he felt it was good to share all that had happened in my life since my incarceration.

I had been to a lot of church services held in correctional facilities. People usually listen politely, and sometimes, maybe one or two men will accept Christ when the invitation is given. I came to the Charlottesville-Albemarle Joint Security Complex as a familiar face. A lot of the men had known me before I had given my heart to God. And they remembered.

I preached to them out of the same Word that had changed my life. When it came time to give the invitation, forty-five out of the sixty men present gave their heart to Christ. I thought it was just an unusual night, but the next time I went, the same thing happened. This was what God had for me. His hand was here and pouring out a blessing.

After I got home from regular work, and after I put the side work in, my wife and I would sit down for hours and write letters to these men. Sometimes we didn't get to bed until about one or two o'clock in the morning, but we kept in touch with each and every one of them.

It was the beginning of something bigger than either of us could have imagined.

Finding Grace

The fairy tale that you hear in a lot of churches is that once you become a Christian, everything is going to be just great, that God's going to come down and take care of all your needs without you lifting a finger. That's a con, a set up. As soon as people begin looking at God in that way, the first time some difficulties come along they say, "Oh, I guess this God-thing isn't working anymore." Then they blame God.

A lot of folks just want God to come in and clean up all the mess in their lives for them. They don't want any challenges in their lives, so when the challenges come, they just roll right on back into their same old lifestyles. There's no endurance in that. God will take care of you, but he wants you to have a foundation and order in your life. We're not in heaven yet. We've got to get a nine-to-five. We have to provide for the family.

One of our biggest enemies in life is ourselves—our wrong desires, our selfishness, our pride, and a lot more. Even as we struggle to get up, those old patterns can knock us back down. Sometimes when I get knocked down, I want to stay down, but as I look to God, he gives me the strength that I don't have, and I get up. If it were just up to me, most of the time I would just lie there.

I believe that I had to go through so much because God had so much in store for me. After I was tested and tempted and God saw that I wasn't going anywhere, he started making provision. Of course God knew that I wasn't going anywhere, but I had to see it.

"Many are the afflictions of the righteous," it says in the Bible, "but the Lord delivers him out of them all." We have afflictions. We get angry. But there's something within those who surrender their lives to Christ that gives them the power to overcome these challenges. There's a power in me that I don't understand and can't fully explain—a power that gives me love when I can't love a person. There's a power in me that is merciful when I can't give mercy myself.

That's the power God gives us—the grace to live life one step at a time. And as I take each step, I continue to see doors open for me more and more.

BRINGING IN

SUSTAINING GRACE

CHAPTER SEVEN

BURNING VISION

Though we were serving our neighborhood, I knew I was also called to serve men involved in a lifestyle of drugs. I was to help them with the same grace and in the same way I had been helped. I had already begun doing that a little in the jails. I spent one night a week there talking to several of the men, teaching them what I had been learning, helping them to know God as I was getting to know him. It was a beginning.

One day John Manzano brought someone to my attention who needed my help. It was Charles Cutchin, a fellow who had once harassed me quite a bit when I was serving time. Out of obedience to my pastor, I went to see him.

When I got to the window where Charles was waiting for me, I saw a big smile on his face. In the course of our conversation, he started apologizing. As a young boy Charles had accepted Christ, but he hadn't lived out that commitment when he got older. When we were in jail together, Charles had a chance to see my relationship with God and my zeal to really know him. That had an impact on his life. Now, instead of the taunting cell mate I had known a few months ago, I was looking at a man who had been changed.

Of course, I told him that I forgave him, but in my mind I had come there to say "hi" and "bye." That was it. After thirty-five minutes, I was on my way home again.

Homecoming

That's when it came to me. Charles was homeless, just as I had been. Charles was rejected by his family because of his lifestyle. The same had been true of me. Looking at Charles' life, it wasn't hard to see my own.

When I got home, I told Joyce about the visit, and about what had been running through my mind on the way home. Charles would be getting out of jail soon, and he did not have a place to live.

"Why doesn't he come and stay with us for a while?" Joyce suddenly suggested.

"Are you sure about this?"

Joyce had heard about Charles from me, but she had never met him. For me, this was a scary situation. This was a man who had spent seven years in the penitentiary and two more in the local jail. He had learned to be rough with people and take what he wanted. Now we were talking about him coming to live in my home.

But Joyce was sure. And I trusted her. This was the same woman who had loved me through my sin, my addiction. Now she was raising our children to be respectable and to honor God. I knew she was protective of the family, most of all the children.

To hear her confidence, I knew this was the right decision. So together we agreed to invite him to come and stay in our home.

Charles called me that night. I had given him my phone number and said he could call me for fellowship and encouragement. When I told him what we had decided, you could hear the excitement in his voice. He just started thanking God that he had a place to go once he was released.

As soon as I got off the phone, I started to pray. The reality of what was about to happen began to set in, and I was scared. But it didn't matter how much I looked at the "facts"; I was sure Charles was supposed to be in my home. Once I accepted that, that's when I had peace.

The day Charles was to move in, I had to be at work by 7 a.m. That meant Joyce had to pick him up from the jail. Still, I had a peace that things were going to be okay.

Charles soon settled into our home. At first he was uncomfortable with the responsibility expected of him. He wasn't used to being responsible, and it was a challenge for him to learn. Thankfully, we found a job for him right away. That was an important step in beginning to walk in this new life.

Charles spent time with us at church, at our weekly home group meetings, at meals— he was a part of everything we did. When Joyce first suggested he move in, she thought it would be for a month or two, but it turned out to be a bit longer than that. Charles would be an extended member of our household for about five years.

He needed that. It was hard, but he had to separate himself from his wife and family for a while. Their lives revolved around parties and drinking, and he knew that was his weakness. While he was with us, he had a chance to see what it meant to follow Christ every day. Not that we were perfect; we just tried to be faithful to what we knew was right.

A Legal Friendship

I worked at Hall's Auto Body Shop for about two and a half years, and by the time I left, a lot had changed. The guys on the shop floor were my friends now. Many had invited me over to their homes. It was a true miracle, and I knew who to thank for it.

Not long after, I met someone who would help point my life and ministry in the next direction.

One night one of the pastors at our church came to the weekly prayer meeting we held at our house, and he brought someone who wanted to meet us. Jim Johnson was a lawyer with one of the most respected firms in Virginia, and he had a heart of compassion. Some time before, Jim and his wife had opened their home to an eighteen-year-old man caught up in the criminal justice system—just one of the many people Jim had seen wander through life without consistent support and guidance.

Jim saw how I had come out of a criminal lifestyle, and how Joyce and I were ministering to inmates and their families, both in and out of the jail. Having walked a similar path with the young man who stayed in their home, Jim understood the need for this sort of multi-faceted commitment to seeing lives changed. He saw success with what we were doing, and he wanted to become involved.

I took Jim to the jail where I preached on Sunday, and then to New Life, where I had gotten a second start. "I'm praying that one day we can do this in Charlottesville," I told him. And Jim started working on it.

Up until then, our ministry was just Joyce and me helping people as we could. But Jim saw a need to take things a step further, to restructure as an officially recognized non-profit organization. He filled out the paperwork, but one thing was missing: We had to have a name.

But what name would communicate what we were all about? There were so many different aspects of what we did. We worked in our neighborhood—doing a lot with children, inviting people to church, sharing what we had with others. We had also begun men's groups—like the one I was involved in for support—in some of the local churches. We also continued our work in the jail.

In the process, bridges were formed—between churches, between people from various racial backgrounds, between inmates and their families, but especially between individuals and God. Everything we were doing seemed to be building a bridge. What better name could we have than "The Bridge Ministry"?

Support Structures

The friendship Jim and I shared went far beyond helping to organize the Bridge Ministry. More than anything, Jim became a close and dear friend, a true brother.

Before I met Jim's family, I remembered seeing a huge Suburban pull up into one of the dangerous, low-income neighborhoods. I was there talking to a couple of guys who had an addiction problem, trying to encourage them to seek help. Out popped a pregnant woman with several small children. Some of the toughest drug dealers in town were along that same street, but she was clearly familiar with the area.

That was Diane, Jim's wife. Like Jim, she became a tremendous encouragement to our family and to the beginnings of the Bridge. Our families spent a lot of time together, eating dinner and just getting to know each other. I was in and out of jobs and still trying to keep the ministry going. Jim shared financially with us out of what he had, and I was able to share with him as well.

When I went to the jail, Jim would come with me. Here we were—a brother from the projects and an articulate, well-paid lawyer—and yet, somehow, we were used in people's lives. As we shared our life-changing experience with God, we saw the need men had to hear that, both from Jim's point of view as well as from mine. Through our lives, they could see that God's Word did change people in very practical ways.

I was also encouraged because I knew Jim believed in me. He didn't look at my background or my abilities. He knew I was seeking to live by the truth, and that was enough for him. It still amazes me to think how God brought us together and taught us how to trust and love one another. What a friend he has been.

In terms of the ministry, it was Jim who helped get us on the right track when it came to good stewardship. He took over the bookkeeping responsibilities and showed Joyce how to keep track of the financial gifts we were now receiving as a nonprofit organization, and how to record the expenditures we made. We knew this was good, but we didn't realize the dividends it would pay in the years to come.

One Sunday, I stood up at church to tell people what was going on with the Bridge. Our local fellowship had been supportive both financially and spiritually. After church, I was approached by someone who introduced himself as Mickey Moore. Mickey, as it turned out, was an award-winning graphic designer. He offered to give his time and skills to help us, and he was excited to be involved. Within a few weeks, Mickey had pulled together our first brochure, and we started passing them out.

Turned In

In the midst of all this success and progress, we were still severely lacking in finances, both for our family as well as for the ministry. The Commonwealth Attorney's office was trying to put me in jail for not paying enough restitution. I was making about $397 per week at the time, and after I paid child support, bad check debts, and other obligations, I was only bringing home sixty three dollars a week from my regular job.

In order to pay our bills, I worked weekends and nights when I could. I was determined not to go back to selling drugs, and I believed what God's Word said—that he would provide for me if I would live right and be honorable before him. Sometimes the extra work wasn't there, but things would still work out financially. Sometimes groceries would just appear on our doorstep. Our church family helped out a lot. I know within my heart that God was honoring his Word in my life.

The court had only given me a limited amount of time to pay off my fines, and I wasn't going to meet the deadline. When I went before the judge to explain myself, he was pretty upset. But not at me. He turned to the Commonwealth's Attorney and the parole officer.

"Why are you bringing this man before

me?" he questioned. "He is doing all he can to pay off his debts. Plus, he's using his extra time to help others."

The case was dismissed. I can tell you that I would have quit many times if I didn't have so many supportive people on my side, people like Jim and others. They were a strong source of hope. I needed something tangible. I needed God's compassion, support, mercy, and forgiveness to be shown through his people all around me.

That gave me enough strength to move into the next year. I didn't understand that the battle was a long way from being over. My goal had been to become a good husband and a good father, but I was also called to love people who had been rejected.

I saw the provision, blessing, and grace, but I also saw the opposition. At times it was a struggle for me to trust people and trust God. I had grown up with lies and distrust—convinced I had to look out for myself. Now I had to learn to be still and know that there was someone greater than myself. I would win these battles not by turning inward, but by looking upward, and I was determined to keep my eyes on the goal.

Turned Away

Jim and I began meeting with people one-to-one, sharing with them the vision of the Bridge Ministry. One thing we kept coming back to: we needed a place where men could live and be trained in how to live a new life. After prayer, we began pursuing the old Blue Ridge Hospital, a facility just outside Charlottesville with several acres, owned by the University of Virginia. To develop and present a proposal to them, Jim helped gather an advisory board of several local businessmen.

The process was amazing. The series of meetings we had as an advisory board brought together many Christian leaders in our community—men known for their integrity as well as their financial successes. All in all, a foundation was being laid for something far beyond what we had imagined.

As I spent time at the old hospital, I remembered that it had once served as a rehabilitation facility for alcoholics and drug addicts. Looking at the buildings, I began to get a greater understanding of how such a place would function. I could see all the aspects of what we were looking for in the

Bridge Ministry represented right here in these buildings. There was even a chapel on the grounds, a beautiful stone chapel with a lovely paneled interior.

I was also now visiting the jail about two or three times a week, sometimes with a group, sometimes on my own. There were challenges and temptations we had to face every day, but my wife and I were determined not to return to our old ways.

I longed for more support from our local church, but their focus seemed to be on missions to third-world countries. Even though I had a burning desire to reach out to our neighborhood—the neighborhood where the church building stood—I started giving up.

One day our church was having a congregational meeting about buying some property in Haiti that would help the missions work in that needy country. All I could think about was Jesus' words to his disciples: "You will be my witnesses in Jerusalem, and in all Judea and Samaria, and to the ends of the earth." Jerusalem was where the disciples lived. To me, that represented the pattern God had for ministry. We cannot minister in other places while ignoring the place we live.

I stood up and addressed the congregation. "I'm all for the Haiti project. Let's give them the money and let them build what they need to build.

"But what about our community? How can we say we're a community church when we're not involved in our own community?"

Some people were offended by what I said, and for a while it caused some strain in a number of relationships. I didn't realize at the time that their community ministry was not to reach out to our neighbors, but to reach out to me. I was the one God had brought to them. Through me they would sow a seed. They would pour out their lives and their love into me, my wife, and my children. We would be the ones to represent their love and concern to our neighborhood.

I had always been thankful for the church we attended. They had been the folks who had embraced me and my family when we were just beginning to live this new life, but now—because of the tension over what I had said—it was becoming difficult to stay. It made me want to go somewhere else and start over. But that was not God's way, and so again, I gave in to his will.

Celebrating Hope

As a ministry, we were still very much tied to New Life, and we helped several people in the jail "bridge over" to the program there. We didn't recommend just anyone. We were careful to choose men in whom we could see a commitment to change. A local physician, Dr. Greg Gelburd, gave the men free physical examinations and the required routine tests before they entered New Life. He also took time to encourage them and talk with them about the changes ahead in their lives—but, as so often happens, Greg found himself encouraged by these men as well.

More and more people were beginning to come alongside Joyce, me, and the Bridge Ministry board in this new venture. We decided it was time to have a celebration for all that God had done and again share the vision he had given us. We held the meeting at a local church. Five men who had come through the Bridge Ministry told their stories, and there were an additional forty-five men from New Life who also attended.

Almost all of the two hundred people in attendance were from outside our local church, and some were not from any church at all. Many came because of a need in their own families. Many of them we had never even met. We were encouraged to see how God had "blueprinted" the Bridge Ministry in so many people's hearts. He was bringing together something that was beyond our imaginations. He was giving us a glimpse of what the Bridge would become—bringing people together from different backgrounds and different situations to help encourage and support each other through the good times and the bad.

That gathering did give us a lot of hope, but it was personally disappointing because there had been so few from our own church who had attended. I believed that the vision God had given me required their support to succeed. Now, I was confused because I felt like the remarks I had made about ministering to our community had caused a lot of tension. It seemed I no longer had the backing and blessing of my home church.

From what I could see, the vision was dead, even though I continued to be overwhelmed with compassion for those in jail, for those trapped in a lifestyle of drugs. I felt frustrated and rejected. All of those old wounds that had been buried down inside of me were reopened: *I'm not good enough. I'm alone. I've been abandoned by those who were supposed to love me.*

I stopped going to a lot of the groups I had attended. Though I continued to go to Sunday services, I let my hurt separate me from others in my church. Where would I find the support and friendship I needed so much?

An Unexpected Call

When I picked up the phone one day, I heard the voice of someone I didn't imagine or even hope I'd ever hear from again, the judge who had sentenced me—Judge Jay Swett.

Like me, Judge Swett had been discouraged. He had been trying to show mercy, and it seemed to be slapping him back in the face. He had just recently given someone a second chance, and they were soon back before him in court.

"I'd like to see just one of these men be successful," he remarked out loud to a sheriff's deputy one day.

"I know of someone, Judge," the deputy

replied, "and he gives you the credit for making it happen."

The day he phoned, Judge Swett invited me to his office. Now that was a first for me! I had been before a lot of judges, but I had never sat down and chatted with one of them in his office! In the back of my mind, I wondered if this was a set-up.

For the first few minutes, I was very uncomfortable, but as we talked, I discovered that Judge Swett was really interested in my thoughts on a topic of concern to him. He was disturbed at how much separation there was in our community, particularly along racial lines. He and a number of other men at his church were interested in finding some answers. What could they do to make a difference? As part of the answer, he invited me to attend a weekly men's meeting at his church.

The next Monday morning, there I was sitting around a table at First Presbyterian with several leaders from our community. I could see they had a new zeal to reach out to Charlottesville and were searching for spiritual answers to accomplish their goals.

For the first two or three times we met, I

just sat there and didn't say a word. I felt I was there to build a relationship with these men, not to offer them answers. We talked about issues and politics and a little bit about God. At the end of our time, someone would always ask, "How does God's Word tie in to all of this?"

There was a humility here that was clearly from the Lord. We met each other where we were. They always made sure I understood the conversation without making me feel inferior in any way. For the first year I was with these men, I was very careful how I presented my understanding of God. I didn't want to be overbearing. Even when they asked me something directly, I phrased my response as a question.

I never wanted them to be uncomfortable talking about black/white racial issues. I felt that I was tailor-made for that group, just to be there for that time.

We didn't push each other. Over time, we learned how to respect each other. We were there to grow together, to be examples of what the Word of God said Christian fellowship ought to be.

Loving Haiti

Ironically enough, just like my home church, First Presbyterian supported a ministry in Haiti, and they invited me to go with them to help build a missions base there.

Having a drug charge can make it very difficult to get a passport. But thanks to some of my new friends and, I'm sure, their testimonies to God's faithful grace in my life, I was given permission to travel.

Haiti is more than a thousand miles away from Charlottesville, but when I stepped off the plane, I was in a familiar place. I immediately recognized the despair, the poverty, and the anger. The airport—an old, run-down facility surrounded by barbed wire and troops from the U.S. Army Reserve—looked like a battle zone.

We had to pay a couple of Haitians a few coins to take our luggage fifty yards to the truck. We didn't need the help. That was just part of the economy there. Out on the street, I saw a young boy about fifteen to twenty feet away. He had taken the rope around his waist and knotted it many times, hard into his stomach, to try and take away his hunger pangs. He probably had not eaten for days.

Suddenly I was fourteen again, standing on the streets of Charlottesville, looking for the right road to take, looking for my next meal. I stared at the boy and began weeping, not so much for the boy I saw before me, but for the boy that was still in me—a boy who was rejected, hurt, and in pain. That child needed help and he needed grace. He needed to be healed.

As I stood with tears in my eyes looking at that reflection of myself, Jay reached over and put his hand on my shoulder. I knew then that I had someone who understood. My judge was becoming my friend.

Provision for the Vision

The entire week I was in Haiti, I saw many examples of the life I had once lived. The men around me who had come on this missions trip were shocked and saddened that people could live in conditions like that, but I identified with those people.

And I saw something else. In that depth of poverty and with that lack of resources, I saw a God who was working things out with these individuals, changing and transforming their lives for the Kingdom. And I felt like God spoke to me then and said, "That's what I want to do with you."

Why didn't I give up? I couldn't. Not because I didn't want to. I wanted to plenty of times. But God wouldn't give up. He wouldn't give up on me, and he wouldn't give up on the vision he had for my life.

I just couldn't get away from it. God wouldn't let me go. He had called me to this, and he was determined that I see it through. I became fully convinced that this vision was not my own.

The vision of God has nothing to do with you. Even when you don't have any strength, God will pick you up and carry you. My vision was for those who don't know God. I would weep as though they were a part of my own family. I knew these prayers were not from my own heart, but from the heart of God. I prayed that God would give me an opportunity to help those who wanted to change their lives.

That is where God's heart is too. When our will lines up with his vision, it's like hooking up a power line to the main source. I was dead, but the power of God in me was and is very much alive.

I think a lot of times we get confused when it comes to the vision and plan God has for us. We think that because the vision is given to us, that it's our vision. It never was. In fact, we're often blind to the vision as God sees it. The vision was his to start with, and he will see it through. He will provide for it. Where he has given a vision, he will make provision.

That doesn't just mean financial or material supplies. It includes the perseverance we need to make it through, the faithfulness, the patience, the time, the energy, even the "want to"— especially when we haven't a clue as to what he is doing.

Yes, we need to cultivate our life together with God. We need to serve him and honor him. But we should not take ownership of the vision. We are just laborers among many, and we should just let God use his vision to bring change into our lives. As we do, we'll discover that other people will want to change too. That's what I started to see, the farther along we went.

CHAPTER EIGHT

KNOCKING ON DOORS

When we left for Haiti, those of us who attended the Monday morning meeting at First Presbyterian were becoming close friends. When we returned, the bond was even stronger. Given my background, it had never been easy for me to trust people, but that was changing. Our love and support for each other was growing.

When I came home, there was a surprise and a challenge waiting for me. Joyce was in a lot of physical pain. I took her to the hospital where we discovered that she needed an urgent operation. For support, I called Gary Greene, one of the men in the group to tell him what was happening.

"Does the ministry have health insurance for you?" Gary asked.

"No," I answered.

"Well," he said, "I'd like to help you out with the bill. I'm pretty sure that some of the other men in the group would like to do the same."

The doctor that was recommended to us happened to be a member of First Presbyterian also. About two days later, Joyce was able to have the operation she needed. Afterward, several of the men's wives came over to visit her, bringing us dinner, bringing Joyce flowers, making sure our kids could get back and forth to school. And we never had to worry about the bill.

Again, I saw God's Word being put into action through their lives. They came together, focusing on the needs before them, not seeking anything in return.

After that, we started meeting every Thursday for lunch at the church. It was there that I had the opportunity to begin sharing the vision God had given me for the Bridge Ministry and our current pursuit of the old Blue Ridge Hospital. They began to spread the word among the church members, the missions board, and the church elders.

They were interested in supporting us financially, but first they appointed one of their elders, again, Gary Greene, to take a look at every aspect of the Bridge Ministry over the coming two years. Because of the principles Jim Johnson had helped us establish, we were ready for this kind of scrutiny. Things were moving ahead one step at a time, and Gary became a big part of that. He invited his friends to take a look at what we were doing and to become involved as well. He gave of himself in so many ways.

Constructive Criticism

Another one of the elders at the church who had been attending the prayer meetings and Thursday lunches was a fellow named Jack Stoner. From our first meeting, I recognized Jack's confidence and intelligence. Jack and his friend, Mike Cernik, were co-owners of a successful construction company.

Mike and Jack employed about thirty-five people in their business, and in many ways the two were like fathers to them. There was a genuine concern for their employees' well-being, not just while they were working for the company, but even if they were to move somewhere else. Jack and Mike wanted to make sure these men had marketable skills wherever they chose to work. They set up basic classes in carpentry, plumbing, and other specific aspects of construction—all to help train each worker to be the best he could be.

Jack had grown up in the mixed-up days of the sixties, but he had managed to gain a focus and turn his zeal toward the construction business. In many ways, our backgrounds gave us a lot in common. Most important, both of us had a growing relationship with Jesus Christ.

Mike and Jack were men who understood order, and that was something I was still looking for in my life. I shared with them about my relationship with God, and they helped me understand how to build structure into my daily life.

Jack, in particular, helped teach me social skills for the new setting in which I found myself. He had learned so much from his own experience and had an amazing rapport with people. Once again, God gave me new friends who really cared about me. He was continuing to change my life in ways that amazed me.

Beyond Me

Not long after we returned from Haiti, I was talking one Monday morning about my hope to have a place where men could grow in their faith as well as in their work skills— all while living in the community. After the men left the residential program, this would be a transitional step to living on their own again. Jack's partner in business, Mike Cernik, spoke up.

"We've got a house you can use," he said.

Mike and his wife, Irene, owned an unoccupied rental house and were interested in putting it to good use.

This was good news, but it was the cart before the horse. We still hadn't found a place to start the residential program, and now here we were being offered a place for the "follow-up." Even though this didn't follow our expectations, after praying about it, we decided to investigate.

Not long after, we drove to a neighborhood not far from a low-income housing project. Just beyond a park and playground area, we came to a single-story house with a roughly finished basement. It definitely needed some work, and we wasted no time. Over the next few weeks, we hauled a dump-truck load of trash away from the house. About thirty volunteers came over to lend a hand in one way or another, evidence of continued support there, despite the conflicts.

Mike and Irene provided all the materials that were needed and personally gave the kitchen and bathroom a new makeover. I had started my own painting business several years earlier, so I brought my crew over to sand and varnish the floors, paint, and put a new roof on. In about a month's time we were finished. The outside and inside were remarkably improved and ready for the first residents. We called it the Intern House, a name we felt described the process that the men who lived there would be going through, much as a new doctor gets trained for the real world by working and learning from those more experienced. My pastor came over to dedicate the new house to the Lord's work.

Then the challenge came. During the renovation process, one of the neighbors stopped by and asked one of the guys what we were planning on doing with the house.

"It's going to be a jail ministry," he said bluntly.

Alarmed at his answer and not waiting for any details, the neighbor spread the story that there would soon be violent criminals living in their neighborhood. Before long, the phone rang at Mike and Irene's house. Then my phone rang.

"We need to talk," Mike said.

Good Neighbors

"I see this as a spiritual attack," I shared with Irene and Mike at their house later on. "Something good is about to happen in that neighborhood as well as in the lives of the men who will be living in that house." After I left, Mike and Irene seemed to have a peace about what was going on, but there was still a huge hurdle to clear.

The neighborhood had called a meeting in the park just across the street from the house in order to protest the Bridge Ministry coming in. Legally they could not stop it. It would be just a few guys living in a rented house, but we wanted to have their support. Thankfully, we were invited to the meeting too.

I explained to the neighbors that this vision for the Intern House was not just a last-minute idea. The Bridge Ministry had been active for several years now, and this had always been part of the vision.

I also set their minds at ease about the

types of people who would be living there. These would not be men who had committed violent crimes. This ministry had started in my own home with my own kids. These were the kinds of people who had been around my five-year-old daughter and my two-year-old son. Moreover, our desire was not just to see change in the men who would be living there. Our hope was also that we could help the neighborhood in some way to combat their drug problems.

There were still a lot of questions. Finally, one of the neighbors spoke up. Her son, she said, was in that cycle of drugs and jail. "Nothing else is working for them," she concluded. "Let's give this a try."

When we left the meeting we didn't have their undying support by any means, but we had what we needed right then: an open door.

Rough Neighbors

After Charles Cutchin lived with us for about three years, I sent him to New Life for Youth in Spotsylvania, the facility where I had been. I felt like he needed more structure in his life, and he found it there. After about a year and a half, he joined the staff at New

Life and became the assistant director of the program, then returned to live with us for another two years. When we started the Intern House, he moved in to be the onsite director.

There were three men living there in addition to Charles. We didn't have to worry about finding anyone work. There was plenty to do in my painting business. But there was another troubling issue that needed to be dealt with.

A drug dealer lived in the house directly across the street. Even the park where the neighborhood meeting had been held was the site of a lot of drug activity, especially at night. We began praying faithfully that God would show us how to approach this.

Because of my previous lifestyle, I had an indirect relationship with some of the drug dealers, so I decided to approach one of them face-to-face. "We want the drug dealing out of this community," I told him.

His first response was to deny that there was anything going on.

"Look," I said. "Our purpose is to try and help these guys get away from this lifestyle, and your presence is making it difficult."

We wanted to change the neighborhood, and I invited him to be part of what we were doing.

The dealers knew of our relationship with the men in jail and their families. In their own way, they respected what we were doing. A number of them left. Some were arrested. One man started coming to the Intern House for our prayer meeting, and he accepted Christ as his Lord and Savior.

Within about five or six months, that neighborhood was a different place. A peacefulness had settled over it. Kids began playing in the park again. Today, it's a community of people growing together.

Monday Morning, 6 a.m.

One of the most important things we did at the Intern House was pray. Every Monday morning at 6 a.m., a group of men came together to spend time with God. The group of men was amazing in its diversity: African Americans and whites, rich and poor, business professionals and blue-collar workers, lawyers and former criminals, men from different churches and men from no church at all.

When you walked through that door, that

meeting gave you hope. Regardless of how busy any of us were that week, on Monday morning we were there. Men would drive half an hour to get there. I remember a teenager getting up at five o'clock in the morning to make it to the meeting. People were faithful, but most important, God was faithful to meet us there.

When we bowed before God in prayer, we knew he was right there, hearing every word we said. We supported each other, cried with each other, and listened to each other. But it was God who did the work.

I could look around that room and just be amazed at what was happening. This was so far beyond what I had ever imagined God would do. This was never my understanding of the vision he had given me, but it was clearly in his plan all along. I was not to minister just to those in jail, but to those who found themselves in other types of bondage— to their success, to their lifestyle, to their social image.

Many of these men were so different from me. They had grown up with a high degree of formal education and wealth. Yet their need for God was as great as mine.

Where was God taking this ministry? I wasn't exactly sure, but I soon found myself having to keep things on track as best I could.

Down to Business

Overnight we had gone from a mom-and-pop ministry essentially managed and directed by Joyce and myself, to an organization with a board of very influential and financially successful businessmen and women. Although a few on the board understood the vision for the Bridge Ministry, there were a lot who didn't. They were trying to reach ministry goals through their own understanding of business and finance.

Thankfully there were men around me who had patience. Jack and Mike understood that God had brought the board together so that their experience might enhance what God had given me. "You have to bring the board along with you," they encouraged me. "You have to be patient with them while they grow."

Nothing could have been more painful for me. I had a burning desire to witness to men whose lives had been enslaved by life-controlling problems, but once again I was being called to witness to men in the upper levels of society. Other than coming out of the bondage I had with my own extended family, this was perhaps the hardest thing I had to do. I had to be retrained. I had to somehow refocus my energies to do what seemed like a distraction and a delay from my real purpose.

One day I remember one of the board members saying, "We need a vision." A vision? I wondered. God has already given the vision. What are they talking about? It seemed a lot easier to go back to doing the Bridge Ministry by myself with Joyce's help. But that would have been moving backward. God had brought me through that stage. He had accomplished what he wanted to. Now it was time to move on to the next level.

To help hold me to the task, God clearly impressed upon my mind a story from long ago. They were the words Peter spoke to Jesus when many of Jesus' followers were leaving him because of some hard words he had said. Jesus asked him, "What about you, Peter? Are you going to leave?"

Peter responded, "Where else could I go, Lord? Only you have the words of eternal life."

I was seeing a battle with the board that I felt like I could do without, but I needed to see the board through the eyes of God. I saw a board that didn't really understand the vision, and that was getting in the way of progress. But when I saw them through God's eyes, I saw a group of people who really wanted to help, who were trying to be a blessing to this ministry.

Some of them wanted the presence of God that they felt so strongly. My eyes again had to be opened to see that this vision was much bigger than the guys in the jail, bigger than what I was seeing. I began to wonder how many more of these kinds of men God would send me. Instead of being frustrated, I tried to look forward to what God was going to do next.

But what happened next just confused me even more.

Grounds for a Camp Meeting

One day I got a call from the chaplain's office at the jail.

"Somebody has already started a ministry like you're trying to do," the chaplain told me. "It's down in Buckingham."

This I couldn't understand. Buckingham was one of the counties just south of us. Why would God direct me to do something when somebody else was doing the same thing right nearby?

I asked the guys who had been going to the jail with me to come to Buckingham and see this ministry. It seemed like we drove forever, but when we finally got there, we were amazed.

This was a campground owned by the Pentecostal Holiness church. It was a huge place, but it was crowded with run-down buildings and old, rusting trailers. It had a lot of potential, and a lot of trash.

The director of the ministry was leasing the campground from the denomination. He was quite friendly and welcomed us warmly. Over dinner, I asked a few questions to get an understanding of what this ministry was about, and the answers I received concerned me.

When we were by ourselves, I asked the men who had come with me what they thought. There was a mixed reaction. I felt it was important for the director to know that the Bridge Ministry supported him in some way, so we gave him a cash gift.

After we left, I felt my job was just to

watch and wait. Over the next two or three months we heard they were having a lot of struggles. We soon discovered the ministry there was falling apart.

Home Fires

We kept moving forward with our plans and meetings regarding the old Blue Ridge Hospital grounds. We were praying that God would open the door to us for this facility, or point us to another we could use.

I was still dealing with a lot of daily challenges. I was picking up men to drive them to work, going to court to testify for them, and still facing my own financial difficulties at home. The board had agreed to pay me a small stipend each month for my work with the ministry, but there wasn't enough giving to support that commitment. I had begun putting more time into the ministry than the painting business. Even though I was taking jobs on the side, things were tight.

I had to provide for my family, and at the same time I had to be faithful to the calling God had placed upon my life for this ministry. It would have been easy in some ways to walk away from the calling, but I knew that God wanted me to minister to more people than just my family.

My family, though, was at the core of almost everything I did with the ministry. Joyce was a source of strength through her administrative gifts, her prayers, and her encouragement. The kids were so accepting of the men who came through our front door, and they would spend time with us praying for them.

Our home at Riverside had become almost like a halfway house. Sometimes it seemed like we had a twenty-four-hour ministry, and we were growing weary. People were dropping in all the time, with or without calling ahead. The ministry had grown so quickly, it seemed like it was now almost beginning to consume us. We longed for a little peace and quiet to be a family. As the kids were growing older, our little duplex seemed to be getting smaller and smaller. We had been living in public housing for almost eight and a half years now, and Joyce really wanted us to have a home of our own.

It wasn't easy to leave. We had watched that neighborhood change. Before, it had been drug-infested and everyone had kept to themselves. Now people were supporting and loving one another. This was the place we had grown as a family in the Lord, learning to serve and give what we had. Joyce and I felt like we were a spiritual father and mother to the people there, so the idea of leaving felt like we were walking away from our own children.

But there were those who had been with us, growing in their faith and in their leadership. It was their turn to lead now, and it was our prayer that the local church would step in where they were needed.

For us, it was time to move on.

Progressive Leaders

People like progress, but they hate change.

Change, for me, is giving up my own way, giving up my own understanding. Change, for me, is embracing the heart of God.

I had to suffer through change. That may sound dramatic, but it came hard for me. If I wanted God to continue to use me, I had to be willing to let him break me and reshape me. I had to be retrained.

God will use his leaders in mighty ways, but sometimes we are unwilling to be moved to the next level. We get stubborn about things like "the vision" when we are only looking at our own understanding of it. If we're not careful, "the vision" just becomes a substitute for our own ego. We pull in people around us who will agree with us, not challenge us. Instead of seeking God's change, we seek to control.

When that happens, it spells failure for a ministry.

Now it was becoming clear why God named this ministry "the Bridge." This was going to be something that required the unity of the body of Christ to accomplish. It wasn't a one-man show, and I wasn't going to control it. Thank God for that. There was so much still to learn, so many more friends and connections to make.

I think one reason that unity is hard is that it requires each one of us to be willing to change. When we reach that point, God has our attention, and he can change our hearts.

Change also requires something of us that few are willing to offer: humility. If I am always convinced that I am right, that my way is the best way—sometimes the "only" way—then I will never experience the change

God has for me.

The proverb says, "God opposes the proud but gives grace to the humble." To see the unity of the body of Christ, each of us needs to cultivate humility in our lives. Prayer, fasting, worship, service—these are all ways to do this, but none of them will work unless we are open to God's often unpredictable work in our lives.

This is the continuing work of faith and of trust. And it opens the doors to things we could never imagine.

CHAPTER NINE

A HOPE & A FUTURE

After we moved to a new neighborhood, I began to withdraw. With some of the challenges I had faced with my home church, I convinced myself I had a good excuse to disappear for a while. I had always been skeptical of the church because of the things I had seen growing up. Now some of the things that had happened to me seemed to confirm those old feelings. I felt like I really needed a break from church for a while. I wasn't going back to my old lifestyle. I was just tired of church politics. Of course, for me it was just a repeat of the rejection I had struggled with all my life. What had been a minor issue to them was a major issue to me. I kept going to Christ Community in spite of the hurt, because I knew that was my place of safety.

On top of that, nothing much was happening with the old Blue Ridge Hospital idea.

The university that owned the property had not come to any decision. Everything appeared to be on hold. I had been carrying around this idea of reaching out to men and their families for so long, just like a woman carries a baby. Only now I wasn't so sure there was anything to it after all. Was this just something I made up?

The advisory group that had come together for the property search was a real support to me during those days. They kept me going. I trusted them because I could tell they were men of character. Also, I couldn't deny that I had had a real encounter with God. There was no mistaking that. This God thing was real, but what was the next step? Then one day, a thought came to me.

"Let's go back to Buckingham."

I didn't know what to expect exactly. But I can say that I was curious.

When we drove up to the entrance, we saw an old, smoking van pulling out of the driveway. Four or five guys were in it. When they saw us, they stopped.

"Is this facility up for sale?" I asked the driver.

"Yeah," came the reply. "I think they want to sell it."

That's all I needed to hear.

Blinded with Vision

I came back to Charlottesville on fire.

"What about Blue Ridge?" Mike and Jack asked me as I told them about the place in Buckingham being up for sale.

"I know," I said, "but this is the place."

They agreed to go with me and take a look. About a week later, the three of us drove back down to Buckingham. This time, there was a different scene awaiting us. About 350 kids were there attending a youth retreat.

As I stood there and looked over the entire facility, I felt like God showed me something beyond the neglected buildings and grounds, something beyond the physical appearance. I now saw that everything we needed for our ministry was there.

This is where I wanted you all along, he spoke into my heart.

After all these years of waiting and working and wondering, this was what God had in mind. It was too much to take in. I was overcome by God's greatness and love to bring me this far; I just wanted to get on my knees and worship him. I was so thankful for all he had done, and as I thought of the years that had been my life, I was amazed that he would do this for me. He had taken a man out of the gutter and brought me to an incredible place—not just this physical place, but a place in my life where I knew that I belonged and had a purpose.

It was a gift greater than all my dreams, and it was all God's doing. Beyond what I knew or could understand, God's hand had been at work. All along he was connecting me with key people—people I needed to know, people I needed to be able to work with. His vision was never just for my home church alone, but for all who follow him.

But Jack and Mike weren't looking at a palace. What they could see was a run-down facility that was going to take a lot of work to get it usable again. I didn't see any of that now. I was filled with the zeal and the joy of God. I could see that what God had spoken ten years ago might finally come to pass.

Soon after I got back to Charlottesville, we made a phone call to the board of the Pentecostal Holiness church. They agreed to meet with the Bridge Ministry's board at First Presbyterian.

This gave me an opportunity to tell the history of the ministry. I took them all the way back and told them how God had placed this simple word in my heart: "The same grace I have shown to you, the same way, show to others."

"We would like to purchase the facility," I concluded. Now came the dull thud. "But we have no money."

You could almost read their thoughts. Why did we come all this way and spend all this time if these people don't have any money?

"If God wants us to have this place," I added. "I pray he will show it to you."

Then we stopped and prayed, and as I prayed, I felt the presence of God. It rested upon us and brought peace. I believe they felt like we did, that God's hand was with us.

Pretty soon the meeting was over, and the board of the Pentecostal Holiness church had still made no decision. It was in God's hands, just like it had always been.

Reality

A few days later, we got a call. "We believe that God wants you to have this place," they said. They would sell it to us at a fair price, and they were willing to finance it.

We understood that this was the fulfillment of all we had been steering towards. We knew we weren't following something false, something we had created on our own. This whole process had been God's idea, and that brought us much joy.

Not long after the details of the purchase were arranged, reality began to set in. I had not lost the vision by any means, but I had gained a healthy dose of what Jack and Mike saw when they first looked at the campground.

There were seventeen acres hidden away in a beautiful, rural setting. But on those seventeen acres was a huge mess. Besides the limbs and branches all over the ground, there were six run-down, rusting metal house trailers, every one of them infested with snakes. The eight or so cinderblock buildings stood with their doors hanging open, broken windows all the way around. Each was a haven for more wild animals—raccoons, skunks, possums. It was a piece of work.

All in all we estimated it would take about three hundred thousand dollars just to get the place in good enough shape for people to live there. Three hundred thousand dollars! And that didn't even include the purchase price! But my hope was this: that the same God who had brought us to this place was the same God who would see it restored.

Jim Johnson decided to write a grant proposal to a local foundation that cared about the community we lived in. It was the only grant proposal he had written. And they approved it. We received a $110,000 matching-grant opportunity.

I had kept my regular meeting time with John Manzano. Though the church had brought me disappointments, the bonds among us were too strong to ignore. We loved and served the same God, and that's what mattered most. One day, I mentioned to John the opportunity we had with the Buckingham campground. John and I still had different views about our church's outreach in our local community, but his heart had never changed toward these men who needed help, and he suggested I make an announcement about the campground during a morning worship service.

One Sunday I got up and told the congregation what had transpired with the facility in

Buckingham and about the offer from the local foundation. "We have a very unique opportunity," I explained. Those who had supported us all along saw the need, and their response was immediate and generous.

In about one month's time, we received pledges totaling around 25 percent of the remodeling costs. God was continuing to use these people in ways that truly blessed me.

Renewal

We still had a long way to go to meet the challenge, so I started going from church to church trying to raise the rest. In about a month, counting all the pledges made, we had met the matching grant. But even with $220,000 we were still short of what we needed to complete the necessary renovations. Many building-supply companies gave us materials for free or at a substantial discount. I took my own painting crew to Buckingham as well. We spent about six months down there working for free. For these same months, God gave me extra contracting work that I was able to do on the side to pay my workers and support my own family. It was the most profitable work I had ever gotten, and it lasted just as long as we were doing the renovations on the campground.

When Christ Community Church was pledging financial support for the Buckingham facility, we also posted sign-up sheets so people could volunteer to come and work there as well. Groups of about fifty would show up at a time. There was always plenty of work for anyone ready to help. Everything was a mess. There was, of course, a need for plenty of carpentry work, roofing, and painting. We cleaned out bathrooms and the big industrial kitchen, fixed up the beds, and much more. And while people were working, they saw the need for blankets, sheets, and pillowcases, and they came and gave that too.

We were reclaiming this property for God's use. The buildings were constructed well enough to restore, but we tore the six trailers down by hand and hauled them away. Over the course of the next year, we would take nine tractor-trailer loads of junk off that campground. And that included plumbing. There was more plumbing work than you can imagine, and there were no shut-off valves. I remember working in a bathroom when suddenly water just shot up out of the ground like a little geyser! All I could do was look at it.

Home Stretch

As the hard work continued, there were days when it was a struggle to get up, get in my truck, drive the forty-five minutes to an hour, and work down there alone. By then I had put all my savings into this and had donated all that I could out of the painting business. The Bridge Ministry was running out of money, and I couldn't afford to hire anybody else to work with me. Yet we still needed a lot more help. When I didn't have the strength to go on, Joyce would say, "I know God has called us to do this."

They weren't just words. She had given up our resources, had come down to Buckingham so many times with all of our kids, and had worked such long hours. She had said it in so many different ways. To hear her say this, I knew I could keep going.

. With her support, and that of so many others who came to help and encourage, we finished the work. By the time we were done, the place was completely changed. Not only were the buildings in great shape, but through the generosity of others, we had enough food, clothes, and hygiene items for fifty men to live there without bringing a thing of their own.

One day after church, I drove out to Buckingham alone. I got out of my car and stood on the property with tears flowing, thanking God for the endurance and the opportunity to serve in what we now call the Bridge Ministry. As I looked at this property, neatly groomed and put in order, I thought of how God had taken my own life—once rejected and abandoned—and brought me into a place of renewal. I remembered how he had done the same with our old drug-infested neighborhood at Riverside. Here again, God had done the impossible. I was just in awe of his faithfulness.

One at a Time

It was January 2001, and we were ready to fill the campground that God had given us and restored. But instead of the fifty men we had prepared for, we had one. That's right, one.

God, what are you doing? I wondered. We've given everything we've had, all of our energy, all of our finances. I feel like we've done everything you told us to do. Where are the men?

I had gone to New Life for Youth and asked them for some leadership help in starting our program. They had sent five men. Five leaders and one student seemed like a pretty safe ratio, but as it turned out, every one of those leaders had more issues to deal with than the men we were trying to bring in. These were men who could preach and talk about the wisdom and love of God, but they didn't have a foundation in their life for responsible living.

Now I didn't have one person to teach and train; I had six.

And the work had begun.

Confused as I was, there was nothing to do but move forward. God had started this off in this way. This was what he had given us to do.

Eventually, he sent us a second student to join the first, and they bickered the whole time they were there.

It was my responsibility to teach all of these men the most basic things—to love and respect one another, and to be truthful with themselves and with others, no matter how challenging that truth might be. I felt like God had prepared me for this task.

I had wanted God to give me fifty men from the beginning, but he knew I couldn't handle that. I needed to prove myself faithful, to love them, to honor them, to teach them. Before long, there were seven, then eighteen.

Some of the men worked through the program and allowed God to begin to change their lives, and some even went on to live in the Intern House. Others saw God heal their marriages and moved back in with their families. And some of the men we ministered to weren't successful—not yet, anyway. God doesn't give up on us that easily.

God has developed the Bridge Ministry in such a way that when men come to us, no matter how great their mistakes and weaknesses, we are not discouraged from giving them our love and support. I'm not just talking about a "love" that lasts for the twelve to eighteen months of the program. We don't just preach Jesus to them and tell them how they need to live. We become family, holding each other responsible to live rightly just as God has held me responsible through my friendships with others.

What we have doesn't represent a man-made program. It represents our God. Even the physical facility speaks of God's character and of our intentions—we want to be the best in our ministry and in our leadership. Most of all we want to represent our God.

We sanded and varnished the floors, Joyce and I. We didn't just paint them. Even though the men we receive are considered "throw-aways" by society's standards, we see them as valuable. When they come to Buckingham for the first time and see a neat, clean, and order-ly place, they know what is expected of them, regardless of the kind of environment they have come from. They know they need to pick up after themselves, to take a shower. It sets a standard of how to live. That's where our ministry begins. It says to a man who comes to us, "Not only do you belong, but you are welcome and honored here."

Little by Little

Over the first couple of years, we grew from eighteen men to thirty, and from thirty to forty. Several area churches came alongside to support us in various ways. In cooperation with a local businessman, we began to devel-op onsite job training. In addition, we provid-ed a number of opportunities for responsible men in the program to oversee major aspects of the facility, such as meal preparation and grounds maintenance. Now our leadership is "home grown," consisting of men to whom we have ministered.

God has made our ministry simple. It's the same command Jesus gave all his disciples, as recorded in Matthew 28:19, 20a: "Go, and make disciples of all men, baptizing them in the name of the Father, and the Son, and the Holy Spirit, teaching them all things, whatever I have commanded you."

It's a ministry based on grace, an undeserved gift of God—his strength, his vision, not our own. But grace does not come without responsibility, and we want every man to know that and grow with that. We tell them, "You need to be responsible for the things you have done. You need to be responsible to your family. You need to be accountable to your community." These are the things we were taught and we embrace, and these are the things we preach. It was grace for us to be taught how to live productively when we had grown up living the exact opposite. Now we know a little about how to reach others with that grace.

It came clear to me again just the other day. I was in court, testifying on behalf of a man who wanted to get into the program.

"I know that there's a man in there who wants to live right," I heard myself saying to the judge, "but he doesn't know how."

Thank God for his grace when we wanted to live right, but needed him to show us how and be patient while we learned.

Healing Journeys

Our ministry is very simple: we speak to men of the grace of God and show them how to make it real in their own lives. Still, I have had a lot to learn, and that has come in part from others who have been walking this road, or parts of this road, before me. As I have visited other ministries, I have begun to understand a wider view of what God is calling me into for the Bridge. I have begun to see the pieces of the puzzle come together.

I have learned much from John Perkins, an African American minister working in a racially divided community of the "Old South." There, at the Voice of Calvary Ministries in Mississippi, I watched black and white working together and accomplishing a goal, with God's Word and God's love as the basis for their actions. I also saw the fruit of community reconciliation in a place much more divided than our own community.

At Betel, a drug- and alcohol-rehabilitation ministry in England, I saw the importance of building lives in practical ways. I watched Kent and Mary Alice establish a family atmosphere that was truly encouraging. They worked hard to help those in their care to find jobs and gain a sense of responsibility and accomplishment.

At a men's gathering in North Carolina, I saw men coming together because the challenges, the hurt, and the rejection in their own lives had led them to a place of irresponsibility or ineffectiveness as leaders. I watched men confessing their weaknesses and their sins to each other, building new relationships, and receiving new hope through that process.

In my home church, though there were difficulties and tension because of my comments on ministering to our community, I grew to understand the importance of being faithful to a local body of Christ. I learned that others have different gifts and different callings. I learned to see the bigger picture of what God had for this ministry: it was for the larger body of Christ, for a wide diversity of people. In time, I also became an elder at Christ Community Church, and now have the opportunity to serve others in leadership in the ways I have been served and encouraged.

Even my trip to Haiti began a healing process for me. I saw something there that I had kept pushing away—my pain and affliction as a child. As I saw hope in those children who were living without a mother or father, I found a hope to start addressing those issues in my own life.

At each place, God unveiled another part of the strategy for me and this ministry. The Bridge had to start with my wounds, my shortcomings, my weaknesses. God had to first deal with me; then I could become a bridge for others.

Building Bridges

Nothing will ever take the place of that first bridge in my life: the grace of Jesus Christ. God has worked in my life to such a depth that even when the world had given up on me, and my mother and father were gone, when nothing else around me could sustain me, I knew I had God to lean on. I could place in his arms everything I had and loved. I trusted him then, and I trust him now.

I don't look at the bridge before me any more. I look at the bridge behind me, and the bridge behind me gives the strength to cross the one before me. The testimony of what God has done in my life keeps me moving forward in the will of God.

Yes, we've had challenges, new bridges to cross. Walking this path does not mean that my past is immediately gone. As God brings things back to my memory from my childhood, my first reaction is to push them back down. But I've learned that I eventually have to face them, and conquer them. And my hope in doing so is not in my own strength. My hope is in God.

He has even used my weaknesses. I missed so much in the way of formal education, but God has been faithful to bring along people to help me in that area so I can be successful in doing what he has called me to do. The pain and the heartache are there. The challenges are there. But we're not alone. Grace walks with us.

And he is more than sufficient.

CONCLUSION

ONE LAST
THING

At the Bridge we see a lot of men who have a drug or alcohol problem, but that's only the beginning. Just about every man who comes through our program has a life-controlling issue. It may have led to drug or alcohol abuse, or it may have caused other results.

I often start by asking some basic questions: Why did you think it was okay to do drugs? Was it rebellion? What was it about your upbringing? Did you have a father in the house? Or did you have a mother who tried to be a father too? Do you have a problem with respect for authority? If we don't deal with these underlying issues, we can deal with a drug or alcohol problem all we want, but with no results.

For the men around me, their hope often begins with seeing my life, to see for themselves what God has done and continues to do in me and through me. Hope can come in so many different ways.

I wonder where hope is for you today.

The whole reason I've written this book is to talk to people who have come to a point in their lives where they may have lost hope, who feel as if they don't have strength to go to the next level, who can't come out of the addiction or face the challenges of life—people who have been broken, and broken so deeply that the brokenness is stronger than their strength.

I'm saying that there is a God who is able. No matter where you are, if you submit your life to him and trust him, he can bring you out—not necessarily in the way you want it to happen, but in the way that he knows that is best for you.

I have experienced this over and over again, and I still experience it. I understand that this type of healing doesn't stop. I'm learning to walk with God faith by faith and journey by journey, and I've come to find out that once he gets me through one thing, there's always another way in which I need him.

But the grace of God doesn't eliminate my

responsibility in the walk. A man reaps what he has sown. That means that I have to go back to the things I have done and face them. But now I don't face them by myself. When I have come to places where I was so overwhelmed—financially, or spiritually, or physically—I depended on his grace to get me through. And I still do.

So my message to you is this: No matter where you've come from, whatever your background or experiences or problems, my God's grace is sufficient. If you allow him to walk with you in a day-to-day walk, you'll discover that his grace is more than just a story in this book; his grace is sufficient for you . . . today.

my family would be out on the street. Up against all that, I guess I figured it wouldn't hurt to try God.

Almost without thinking, I prayed.

"God, if you are there—I don't know if you are, but if you are—please, please just help me to pay the rent for my family." I was completely serious when I said it, but I'm not sure I expected an answer.

The day after I prayed, I was on my way somewhere when a fellow I knew drove up around the corner.

"Hey," he called, "I've really been looking for you. I've got a car for you to detail. Can you do it?"

I know a lot of people will say that was just a bit of good luck, but not me. As crazy as it may have seemed, I believed God had sent this man to me so I could pay the rent. He had listened to me. It would be a while longer before I knew very much about listening to him.

Cat and Mouse

Because of my addiction, I couldn't keep the money coming in steadily enough through my detailing work, so I went back to what I knew—dealing drugs. Now, of course, I was

CHAPTER THREE

BITS
&PIECES

I can't tell you how disappointed I was when I woke up the next morning—alive. Anger rose up within me. It was torture to look at Joyce and my kids, knowing they didn't have any food. I had to live one more day knowing that I was useless as a father, hopeless as a provider for my family, and a failure as a husband. It was the worst day of my life.

The car detailing work was a losing proposition. Being a drug addict and being responsible just don't go together. I started losing contracts. Soon I was behind on court-ordered restitution payments, not to mention child-support payments from an earlier, broken relationship. Within a couple of weeks, I found myself seriously behind on the rent. If I didn't come up with some money very soon,